Elite Swim Workout '22

Elite Swim Workout 22
Copyright © 2022 Jakub Kalinowski

All rights reserved. This book or any portion thereof
may not be reproduced or used in any manner whatsoever
without the express written permission of the publisher.

ISBN: 9798459747812

All rights reserved.

Check out *the other Elite Swim Workout signature series books:*

ELITE SWIMMING WORKOUT 2019-2020
ELITE SWIMMING WORKOUT 2019-2020 METERS Edition
ELITE SWIM WORKOUT 21

For my two lovely daughters who have just started their own swimming journey.
To all the coaches who I've worked with over the years, who have inspired many of the sets
in here.

Welcome to Elite Swim Workout 22!

Back once again, and this time with more umph.

Before we get started, just the usual note about the author, ie) myself.

Ive been swimming now for 27 years.

Throughout the years, I have practiced with all types of people and teams. Ive
trained and competed against Olympians and gold medalists, triathletes, state champions,
and cut my teeth against some of the fastest swimmers on the planet.
As a teenager, I was a full-on distance swimmer, winning state championships in the
1650. I eventually moved over to mid-D, setting multiple school records in events like 500 ,
200, and the 100.

In college, I joined a D1 school, and transitioned to full time sprinting, breaking numerous school records
(50,100, 200 and all the relays), and eventually becoming a league champion in the 50, setting the 50 free
record for the meet (which was then broken again soon after).
After graduating in 2012, I took a short break, before getting back into it and competing
again at the US Open in 2013.

Swimming is a hard sport, there is no getting around that. Part of the difficulty is the
amount of time that needs to be invested to keep up with ones training. After starting a
family, I found it was quite difficult to find the time to make it to Masters workouts, which
led me to train quite a bit by myself.
That, dear reader, is where this book comes in.
The resources out there are very limited when it comes to workouts for top tier
athletes, especially if you are swimming with no coach. Most training regimes you find
online feel quite random and its impossible to find an Olympic-level workout for
the seasoned swimmer.
That being said, this doesn't *have* to be for an Olympic-caliber athlete. If you find the
times are too fast, use the slower interval listed on the sheet. If its still too much, the intervals
can easily be adjusted by adding 10-20 seconds per set.

All in all, what you'll find here is a season's worth of workouts, for the motivated
athlete. Each has been custom crafted, and they are all reminiscent of the top-tier workouts
I experienced throughout my college career.

Each training session is designed for a specific day for the 2021-2022 college season, and
maintains a single day off per week (Sunday).

Hope you enjoy!

GLOSSARY of TERMS

FR: Freestyle
BK: BackStroke
BR: BreastStroke
FL: Butterfly

JMI: Just Make the Interval
SKIMPS: Swim, Kick, IM, Pull, Swim
200 SKIMPS means 200 swim, 200 kick, 200 IM, 200 Pull, 200 Swim

Choice: Your choice of Stroke
Stroke: Your main Stroke
IM: Individual Medley (Fly, Back, Breast, Free)
IMO: see above
RIMO: Reverse IM Order (Free, Breast, Back, Fly)

Broken: Break the distance per instruction.
(Broken 100 - Break at the 50 for the specified amount)
(Broken 200 - Break at the 100 for the specified amount)
(Broken 500 - Break after each 100 for the specified amount)

These below correlate to your heart rate, but its easier to understand by effort/ speed:
Clear: 0% Easy pace
White: 25% Casual effort
Pink: 50% Half effort
Red: 60-70% Hard effort
Blue: 80-90% Fast pace
Max: 100% MAX pace

Negative split: Second half must be faster than the first half
Build: Slowly raise effort and speed as you go
Accelerate: Max effort breakout + 4 Strokes, rest of the length is easy
Underwater: Swim the length underwater with no breathe

DPS- Distance per Stroke. Try to minimize your stroke count.
BP- Breathing pattern (BP - 5 means one breath every 5 Strokes)
RB- Restriction Breathing (RB:2 Means 2 breaths total for the length)
RB:0- No breath this length

(Multiple intervals)
3:40/4:00/4:20 - - Choose one interval for the set that works for you.
Left most interval is the most challenging.

4 x 200 Free/Back @ 3:00 /3:30 -Four 200's, your choice of Free or back. You pick the interval for the whole set, either 3:00 or 3:30

3 x {ITEM} - The item in the brackets will be done 3 times

(1:00)- One minute rest

Reduce:1 - reduce Stroke count by alloted amount per length.
Best Average: Maintain the fastest speed you can for the duration of the set. For example, 5x100 best average - If the best you can hold is 1:00, then hold that time for the full 5 x 100's
Goal Pace: Take either your goal time for the specific event, or your best time for the event and add the specified amount to it to get your time.

Drills

Descend, D1-4 - Descend your time. D1-4 means the 4th one should be the fastest

Ascend: Start fast and then slow down

Catchup-(Freestyle, BackStroke). Start in streamline position with a steady kick. Perform a front crawl Stroke where your hands touch before the next
hand begins its motion

Heads up - (Freestyle) Keep your head out of the water

Fingertip - (Freestyle) Drag your fingertips on the surface of the water

Single arm - (Freestyle, Butterfly, Back) Only use One arm. Reverse arm on the length back

2K, 1P - (BreastStroke) - Two kicks for every One Pull

Breast w/ DK (BreastStroke) - BreastStroke with Dolphin kick

Breast w/ FK (BreastStroke) - BreastStroke with Flutter kick

Double arm back (BackStroke) - BackStroke with concurrent double arm pull

Fist (Freestyle): Freestyle with a fist rather than an open palm

HOW TO READ THE WORKOUT

Tuesday, September 24nd, 2019

400 Free
200 Kick
400 RIMO
200 (100 Dbl arm back/50 Choice/50 kick)

8 x 50 (25 kick no board/25 swim) @ :100
4 x 75 (25 fist drill/25 swim/25 build) @ 1:20

1.
➤ Warmup (For everyone)

Distance

3 x (500 + 100 easy)
#1 White
#2 Build each 100 to Red
#3 Last 25 of each 100 only 2 breaths

6 x (200 + 50 easy)
#1-2 IM Swim
#3-4 Kick Red
#5-6 Swim Red

10 x (100 + 50 easy)
#1-5 Hold 1000 Goal Pace +3
#6-8 Hold 1000 Goal Pace +2
#9-10 Hold 1000 Goal Pace +1

Sprint

4 x 125 @ 1:50
(75 build each turn, 3 strokes no breath off wall)
6 x 25 accelerate @ :30

15 x 100 @ 1:30/1:40
#1-5 Negative Split (White/Blue)
#6-10 Descend to MAX
#7-15 Hold Best Average

1 x 300
2 x 200 @ 2:40

Mid D Free/Back/Breast

3 x (400 + 100 easy)
Back & Breast (2) W, P
Free 2W,P

4 x (200 + 50 easy)
(50 Kick R, 150 Swim Descend to R)

5 x (100 + 50 easy)
Hold Goal 500 Time +3
Hold 200 Goal Time +2

2 x through
4 x (50 + 50 easy)
Hold 200 Goal Time

2.
➤ After the warmup, Pick ONE category that best fits your expertise. This is your main set

IM

4 x (300IM + 100 easy)
White-Pink
4 x (100(50 Free/50 Fly) + 50 easy)
Free=Pink, Fly =Red
4 x (75 Back + 25 easy breast)
D 1-4 to Blue
    4 x (50 Breast + 50 easy)
Hold Red

Equipment needed:

Swimsuit: Public swim pools strongly frown on nude workouts.

Drag-suit: I swore by one. Slows you down by a small amount. Drag-suit comes off when its time to get serious.

Cap: Keeps your loose hair out of the pool.

Water Bottle w/water: Hydration is key.

Board: Everyone's favorite mid-workout surfboard. Used for kicking sets. And there'll be lots of 'em!

Fins: Get a size that fits, and that won't fall off when you kick hard or do flip turns. I prefer the longer ones over the short fins.

Paddles: Expands the size of your hands, to work on your pull. Get a size that works for your hand, I wouldn't recommend going overboard with the monster sized ones.

Buoy: To put in between your legs and to stop kicking, and for rotations. Bread and butter of swim workouts.

Chutes: Strap it to your waist and significantly increase the resistance you feel in the water. Must have for sprinters.

*All the of the workouts are designed for a standard 25 Yard pool

September 2021

1 Wednesday
2 Thursday
3 Friday
4 Saturday
5 Sunday
6 Monday
7 Tuesday
8 Wednesday
9 Thursday
10 Friday
11 Saturday
12 Sunday
13 Monday
14 Tuesday
15 Wednesday
16 Thursday
17 Friday
18 Saturday
19 Sunday
20 Monday
21 Tuesday
22 Wednesday
23 Thursday
24 Friday
25 Saturday
26 Sunday
27 Monday
28 Tuesday
29 Wednesday
30 Thursday

Wed Sep 01 2021

2 x 300 Pull/ @ 3:45/3:50
5 x 100 Pull (50 Free/50 Non-Free) @ 1:30/1:40

2 x {
   1 x 400 Kick
   4 x 50 Kick w/fins
}
4 x 100 @ 1:15/1:20
4 x 25 DPS @ :25
(:30)
4 x 100 Descend

    SPRINT
10 x 50 kick @ 1:00

1 x 100 Broken @ 25's
1 x 50 MAX
6 x 25
#1-3 MAX breakout
#4-6 build

6 x 100 (50 free/50 kick @ 1:20
4 x 150 choice

    DISTANCE

1 x 600 Kick (300 Kick No board/300 Kick Board)
6 x 50 Kick @ 1:00
#1-3 Worst Stroke
#4-6 Best Stroke
4 x 200 @ 4:50/5:00
White-Pink-White-Pink
2 x 200 IM @ 2:45/3:00
2 x 200's MAX @ 2:30
2 x 100's MAX @ 1:30
4 x 50's MAX @ :50
4 x 25's MAX @ :30

    MID-DISTANCE

3 x 500 (White/Pink/Red)
3 x 400 (White/Pink/Red)
(2:00)
4 x 200 (White/Pink/Red/Blue)
4 x 100 Best Average

Thu Sep 02 2021

3 x 200
#1 Free
#2 (50 BK/50 Breast)
#3 DPS Choice

4 x 200 Kick @ 4:00
50 Kick Pink/50 Kick Red/50 Kick Pink/50 Kick Red
100 Kick Pink/100 Kick Red
100 Kick Red/100 Kick Pink
50 Kick Red/50 Kick Pink/50 Kick Red/50 Kick Pink

4 x 200 (FR/FL by 100's) @ 2:50
8 x 100 @ 1:25
odds: Free
evens: Fly
(2:00)
3 x 200 (FR/FL) @ 2:40
6 x 100 FLY @ 1:40

Fri Sep 03 2021

600 (300 Free/300 Non-Free)
400 Free
200 Kick
200 (100 BK/50 Choice/50 kick)

6 x 50 Fist Drill @ 1:006 x 25 Build to great finish @ :30

2 x {
    1 x 300 Kick (150 White w/board/150 Pink no board) @ 5:45
    4 x 50 Descend to MAX @ 1:00
    4 x 25 Dolphin on back @ :30
}

     SPRINT

1 x 300 White @ 4:00
4 x 50 D 1-4 @ 1:00
4 x 100 White @ 1:40
4 x 50 D 1-4 @ 1:00
200 White

4 x 50 Max Breakout @ 1:30

     DISTANCE
     4 x 200
Pull - Kick - Pink - White
2 x 800
odd 100's: Descend
even 100's Kick Pink
6 x 200
odds: Blue @ 2:20
evens: IM @ 2:40
5 x 100's
(100's Descend 1-5 Red + 25 MAX)

     MID-DISTANCE

1 x 900 (300 fl-300 every other free – 300 stretch drill)
1 x 600 (300 fl/fr-300 back/breast)
1 x 1000 Broken
9 x 100 @ 1:15 BP: 3-5
(10 x 100 @ :20 rest)

Sat Sep 04 2021

6 x 150
odds: Free
evens: Choice

4 x 100 IM @ 2:00
RB:2 on last 25 Free

1 x 600 Paddle/Pull
Bp 5 by 100's work on great turns
1 x 400

3 x 100 Kick @ 1:50
#1 (50 Kick/50 Dolphin Kick)
#2 (50 Breast Kick/50 Flutter no board)
#3 Build each 50 to Pink

4 x 25 Build @ :40

2 x (10 x 50 KICK @ 1:30) ALL OUT MAX

1 x 300 Free @ 4:30
5 x 50 drill Choice @ 1:00

4 x 100 choice @ 1:40

Mon Sep 06 2021

4 x 200 @ :15 rest
odds: IMO
evens: (50 free drill/50 Choice)

20 x 25
#1-10 w/ chutes @ :45
#11-20 MAX w/ fins underwater kick @ :40

SPRINT

8 x 50 MAX Turns Mid Pool @ :50
4 x build @ :30

6 x 50 @ 4:00
#1-2 MAX w/ 2 Breaths
#3-4 MAX w/ 1 Breath
#5-6 MAX w/ 0 Breaths

4 x 25 w/fins from Dive

DISTANCE

6 x 25 (Drill/Build/Drill/Build/Drill/Sprint) @ :40

2x Broken 200's
(:20 secs each 100)

2 x Broken 100 (@ each 50 for :10 seconds)
1 x Broken 100 (@ each 25 for :10 seconds)

4 x 50 MAX @ :40
#1-2 max of 3 breaths
#3-4 max of 2 breaths

MID-DISTANCE

5 x {
   400 @ 4:30/4:45/4:50
   4 x 100 Goal 500 Pace @ 1:10/1:15/1:20
   1:00 rest
   }

Tue Sep 07 2021

200 SKIMPS
8 x 50 @ 1:00
odds: RB:1
evens: RB:3

5 x 50 Dolphin on Back @ :50

12 x 75 Continuous IM @ 1:10
4 x 25 IMO Descend @ :30

4 x 100 Fly @ 1:45

1 x 400 IM @ 6:30
4 x 100 Choice 2 red/ 2 pink @ 1:50
(:30)
1 x 400 free @ 5:00
2 x 100 (2) White (1) Pink
(:30)
1 x 400 free @ 5:00
5 x 100 Fly blue @ 1:30

Wed Sep 08 2021

6 x 150
odds: (Free/Non-Free/Free) by 50's
evens: (100 Kick/50 Breast)

12 x 75 @ 1:10
Fly-Back-Breast/Back-Breast-Free
6 x 100 IM @ 1:50
8 x 50 IMO @ 1:00

    SPRINT

1 x 400 (200 White/200 Pink)
2 x 100 IM @ 2:00
10 x 50 @ 1:00
Odds 50 Free
Evens 50 NonFree

2 x 200's MAX @ 2:30
2 x 100's MAX @ 1:30
4 x 50's MAX @ :50
4 x 25's MAX @ :30

    DISTANCE

2 x 400 Paddle w/Pull Buoy @ 4:45/5:00
3 x 200 IM :30 sec
4 x 50 Free @ :40

2 x 300 (150 Free/150 Non-Free) @
4 x 100 Descend @ 1:30
4 x 50 Free @ :40

4 x 25's Max start + breakout

    MID-DISTANCE

5 x 200 Neg Split @ 3:00
5 x {
   200 @ 2:45/2:50 +
   3 x 100 @ 1:30)
}
3 x 50 Kick MAX @ 1:45

Thu Sep 09 2021

1 x 400 (200 Free/200 Non-Free)
1 x 300 Kick
1 x 200 RIMO (drill fly)

1 x 300 Scull

6 x 75 w/fins (drill/swim/drill) @ 1:10
6 x 75 w/fins (underwater kick/swim/dolphin on back) @ 1:15

4 x 200 @ 2:30/2:40
First 50 build to MAX turn + 3 Strokes breakout no breath
(1:00)
4 x 100 @ 1:25/1:30
(25 no breath Red/75 Choice)

2 x 300 @ 3:40/3:50
#1 Negative Split – White/Pink
#2 Negative Split – White/Red

8 x 100 JMI
#1-4 @ 1:20/1:25
#5-8 @ 1:10/1:15

Fri Sep 10 2021

3 x 600
>   #1 200 RIMO/200 Swim/200 Drill
>   #2 300 (50 drill/50 swim best Stroke/300 kick)
#3 Swim Choice

8 x 50 @ :50
odds: build into first wall, great turn
evens: build into finish, great finish

2 x {
    4 x 25 (drill,build,drill,MAX) @ :40
}

SPRINT

1 x 400 (200 White/200 Kick Red)
2 x 200 (100 Pink/100 Kick Red) @ 3:00/3:10
4 x 100 Descend to MAX @ 1:20/1:40

2 x {
    2 x 100 JMI @ 1:40/1:50/2:00
    2 x 75 Build each 25 to Pink @ 1:15/1:20/1:30
    4 x 50 Red @ 1:05/1:10/1:15
    8 x 25 @ 1:00
    odds: from Dive
    evens: from Push
}

DISTANCE

1 x 1000 Broken
(10 x 100 @ :20 rest)
1 x 500 Broken
(10 x 50 @ :10 rest)
4x 75 Paddle w/Pull Buoy

MID-DISTANCE

20 x 100 @ 1:30
#1-5 Negative Split(White/Red)
#6-20 Best Average

Sat Sep 11 2021

4 x 200 @ :15 rest
odds: Free
evens: (50 back drill/50 Choice)

4 x 200 @ 2:30/2:40
odds: BP: 3,5 by 100
evens: BP: 3,7 by 50
(2:00)
3 x 300 w/fins @ 3:15/3:30
odds: DPS – lowest Stroke count
evens: kick ½ underwater on each wall
(2:00)

5 x {
   200 IM Best Average 2:20/2:40/2:50
   4 x 50 IMO @ 1:10
   1:00 rest
}

Mon Sep 13 2021

200 SKIMPS
Pull- (2 x 25 Choice/75 Swim)

10 x 75 continuous IM @ 1:10

SPRINT

3 x 100 (white/pink/red) @ 1:40
2 x 100 Pink – Red @ 1:30
4 x 50 D 1-4 @ 1:10

25's from a dive MAX
6 x 25 build to max finish

4 x 200 (free/stroke/kick) @ 3:00

DISTANCE

2 x (300 + 100 easy)
Pink – Pink
4 x (200 + 50 easy)
Descend
4 x (100 + 50 easy)
D 1-4
8 x (50 + 50 easy)
Hold Goal 500 Pace

MID-DISTANCE

4 x (200 pull + 100 easy)
Descend

7 x (100 + 50 easy)
#1-5 Goal 500 Pace
#6-7 Hold #5 Time

4 x (50 + 50 easy)
All Fast

Tue Sep 14 2021

200 SKIMPS

8 x 50 Drill @ 1:20
odds: 25 Left Arm Free/25 Right Arm Free
evens: 25 Catchup/25 Stroke

6 x 50 (25 fist/25 pink) @ 1:00
Concentrate on high elbow catch
6 x 50 Free Underwater Recovery Drill @ 1:00

1 x 400 Kick w/fins
5 x 50 Kick w/fins dolphin on back @ :50
6 x 25 underwater MAX kick w/fins @ :25

8 x 200 @ 2:40
#1 (25 Red + 175 White)
#2 (50 Red + 150 White)
#3 (75 Red + 125 White)
#4 (100 Red + 100 White)
#5 (125 Blue + 75 White)
#6 (150 Blue + 50 White)
#7 (175 Blue + 25 White)
#8 200 MAX

1 x 400 (50 Free/50 Non-Free)
8 x 50 KICK D1-4, 5-8 to MAX @ 1:00

Wed Sep 15 2021

2 x 200 #1 Free, #2 Non-Free
4 x 100 IM :20 sec
6 x 50 @ 1:00 2 fist drill, 1 build
3 x 100 Kick @ 1:50

3 x {
   1 x 300 Paddle w/Pull Buoy @ 4:00
   3 x 100 Pull @ 1:30
}
8 x 25 w/fins underwater kick @ :30
4 x 50 w/fins underwater kick @ 1:00
(Max of 1 breath allowed per 50)

   SPRINT

6 x 150 Paddle/Pull @ 2:15

200 Kick

6 x 25 Blue @ :30
10 x 25 Kick w/fins & chutes underwater @ 1:00

   DISTANCE

5 x (300 Best Average @ 3:50 + 3 x 100 Goal 500 Pace −1 @ 1:30 + 1:00 rest)

   MID-DISTANCE

2 x 600 (300 White/300 Kick Red) @ 10:30/10:50
3 x 300 (150 Pink/150 Red Kick) @ 8:40/8:50
10 x 100 D1-5 , Hold time on 5-8, 9-10 MAX

1 x 300 JMI @ 4:00/4:20
2 x 200 Kick @ 4:00/4:20
#1 Flutter #2 Dolphin
4 x 50 Red Swim @ 1:10/1:15

Thu Sep 16 2021

1 x 600 Free
2 x 400 (200 Kick/200 Back)
4 x 100
odds: IM
evens: (50 Breast Kick/50 Swim)

16 x 50 @ :50
#1-4 sprint turns in & out of flags
#5-8 BK 15 yds underwater kick + fast breakout
#9-12 free with fast kick
#13-16 Fly 25 kick/25 fast

5 x {
   200 IM Best Average @ 2:20/2:40/2:50
   4 x 50 IMO Avg B.T. 200 Pace
   1:00 rest
   }

Fri Sep 17 2021

1 x 600 (300 Free/200 Kick/100 Breast)

1 x 500 Kick

8 x 25 w/fins FAST underwater kick @ :40
1 x 400 Kick White @ 7:00
4 x 50 (25 Blue/ 25 white) @ :50

SPRINT

8 x 100 w/fins Fast kick @ 1:30
odds: Flutter
evens: Dolphin
4 x 50 D 1-4 @ 1:00
8 x 25 MAX From Dive

DISTANCE

1 x 400 (100 Free/100 Back)
2 x 200 Stroke @ 2:30/2:40
Pink – Red
4 x 50 (12.5 underwater MAX kick + MAX breakout/12.5 easy swim) @ 1:00

2 x {
   1 x 25 MAX from Dive @ :30
   1 x 75 JMI @ 1:10/1:15
   1 x 50 kick ½ way underwater on every wall @ :40/:45
   1 x 25 MAX underwater kick from Dive @ :40
   1 x 100 MAX for time
}
6 x 100 @ 1:40

MID-DISTANCE

1 x 400 Build each 100 to MAX flip3 x 200 Red @ 2:30/2:40
4 x 150 (100 Build to Pink + 50 Red)

3 x 100 (50 Kick/50 Swim) @ 1:40

Sat Sep 18 2021

4 x 200
Free - Choice - Back/BR by 50's-Kick

3 x 100 Non-Free work walls @ 1:40

6 x 50 Fist Drill @ 1:00
6 x 25 Build @ :30

1 x 200 Work breakout on each wall @ 3:00
4 x 50 Dolphin on Back @ 1:00
4 x 25 Build @ :30

3 x {
   1 x 25 MAX :30 rest
   1 x 50 MAX Kick :45-1:00 rest
   1 x 50 MAX Dive
}
1 x 500 Free
5 x 50 Non-Free @ :50

Mon Sep 20 2021

3 x 200
#1 Free
#2 (50 BK/50 Breast)
#3 DPS Choice

8 x 50 @ 1:00
odds: fast turns
evens: build to fast finish

    SPRINT

8 x 75 Paddle w/Pull Buoy @ 1:15

4 x 25 (drill,build,drill,sprint) @ :40

2 x Broken 100 @ 25's
200 easy

6 x 100 (swim/kick/non-free/Choice) @ 1:40
10 x 50 @ 1:40

    DISTANCE
8 x 50 build to great finish @ 1:00

1 x 300 MAX
3 x 100 MAX @ 5:00

10 x 50 @ 1:00
Odds 50 Kick
Evens 50 Swim

    MID-DISTANCE

10 x 50 @ 4:00
#1-3 MAX of 3 Breaths
#4-6 MAX of 2 Breaths
#7-10 MAX of 1 Breath

4 x (75+ 25 easy)
Descend
8 x (50 + 50 easy)
Round 1 all red
Round 2 all MAX

Tue Sep 21 2021

1 x 400 Back
2 x 100 Freestyle

6 x 75 w/fins (25 underwater kick/25 swim/25 underwater kick) @ 1:20
(1:00)

3 x 200 Free @ 2:30 D 1-3
4 x (100 Fast + 50 easy)

3 x 200 Paddle/Pull
6 x 50 max of 2 breaths @ 1:00

8 x 200 IMO @ 2:40

15 x 100
odds: Free @ 1:20
evens: IM @ 1:30

Wed Sep 22 2021

200 SKIMPS
6 x 50 IMO @ 1:00

8 x 100 (25 Build/50 Pink/25 Build to Fast Finish) @ 1:40
8 x 50 @ 1:00
#1-3 (1/2 underwater Kick + breakout on each wall)
#4-6 Build max of 3 breaths
#7-8 DPS

SPRINT

4 x 25 MAX Breakout @ :30
4 x 50 no breath in or out of wall @ 1:10

2 x (10 x 50 @ 1:30) ALL OUT MAX

DISTANCE

12 x 25 (drill/build/drill/sprint) @ :40
3 x 200 White/Pink/Red @ 2:20/2:30/2:40
6 x 100 @ 1:25/1:30
odds: descend to MAX finish
evens: ascend MAX breakout
6 x 50 MAX each breakout off both walls @ 1:00

MID-DISTANCE

6 x 200 @ 6:00
4 x 200
odds: Free @ 2:30/2:40
evens: IM @ 2:30/2:40

8 x 50 Stroke
#1-4 @ :40/:45
#5-8 Red @ :35/:40

Thu Sep 23 2021

600 Free
3 x 100 Kick w/Board
10 x 100 IM Order @ :15 rest

3 x { w/fins
    25 underwater kick @ :30
    50 Back descend @ :50
    75 Fast Kick - Flutter @ 1:00/1:10
    100 FAST @ 2:00
    }

IM
4 x 200
White-Pink-Red-Blue
(1:00)

2 x (300 + 100 easy)
Pink-Red
(1:30)
8 x (100 + 100 easy)
odds: Free Descend

Evens: Stroke D2-8 to MAX
Cooldown

Fri Sep 24 2021

200 SKIMPS

1 x 400 Paddle w/Pull Buoy @ 5:10
8 x 50 Pull (2 best Stroke, 1 Free) @ :50/1:00

4 x 100 IM (drill fly) @ 2:00/2:10
4 x 50 Back @ 1:00
6 x 50 (25 Breast Kick on Back) @ 1:10
4 x 75 (Free/NonFree/Free) @ 1:10
4 x 25 Breast @ :40

SPRINT

1 x 400 Free Bp 3,5 by 100
6 x 100 Non Free @ 1:45/1:50

2 x {
   1 x 400 IM @ :20 rest
   4 x 100 Free Descend @ 1:30
}
2 x {
   2 x 300 (100 Free/100 Non Free/100 IM) @ :15 rest
   4 x 100 (50 Free/50 Non Free) @ 1:40
}

DISTANCE

12 x 50 JMI @ :35/:40
Build each 50 to Pink – no breath from flags to wall on finish

MID-DISTANCE

4 x 400 IM
(pink - red - blue - max for time)

Sat Sep 25 2021

1 x 600 (200 Free/200 BK/200 BR)
1 x 400 (200 Kick/200 Choice)
1 x 400 Paddle w/Pull Buoy DPS

6 x 150 Kick w/fins @ 1:45
(1:00)
8 x 50 Kick no board @ 1:00
D1-4,5-8

6 x 200 @ 3:00
(White-Pink x 3)
5 x 100 JMI @ 1:10/1:15
4 x 200 (100 White/100 Build) @ 2:40
(1:00)
4 x 100 @ 1:40
4 x 100 Descend @ 1:20/1:30

Mon Sep 27 2021

300 FR
200 Kick
100 IM
1 x 500 Paddle/Pull

50 Kick @ :10 rest
100 Free @ :10 rest
200 non-Free @ :10 rest
300 Kick @ :10 rest
200 Fin Swim @ :10 rest
100 Free @ :10 rest
50 Worst Stroke @ :10 rest

SPRINT

4 x 100 (50 Drill/ 50 build to max finish) @ 1:30

1 x Broken 200 @ 50
2 x 100 MAX
Cool Down

DISTANCE

2 x 300 White- Pink @ 3:50
3 x 100 Descend @ 1:30
8 x 100 Negative Split @ 1:40
4 x 50 D 1-4 @ 1:00
4 x 100 White BP:5 by 50's @ 1:30
10 x 100 Build to great finish @ 1:20

MID-DISTANCE

4 x 200 choice @ 2:40/2:50
(1:00)
4 x 150 (50 White/100 build) @ 1:50/2:00

20 x 100 Maintain best average @ 1:20/1:30

1 x 400 Free easy
5 x 100 Kick MAX @ 2:00

Tue Sep 28 2021

1 x 400 Free
1 x 200 Kick with board
3 x 100 Freestyle

12 x 75 @
#1-4 (50 Free/25 BK)
#5-8 (25 Kick no board/50 Breast)
#9-12 (Fly/Back/Breast)

4 x 200 Paddle/Pull

8 x 50 @ :50

1 x 200 w/fins
4 x 50 @ 1650 Pace @ 1:00
1 x Broken 500 @ 100's for :10 rest
4 x {
    4 x 100 Neg Split @ 1:30
    (White/Pink)
    4 x 50 Descend
    4 x 25 Build
}

Wed Sep 29 2021

4 x 300 paddle only BP 3-5-7 by 100's
4 x 200 Fin Kick @ 2:45
4 x 100 Fin Kick @ 1:20

3 x {
   300 Non-Free @ :20 rest
   200 Swim – Pink @ 2:30
   100 Swim – Red @ 2:00
}

    SPRINT

1 x 25 MAX from Dive @ :30
1 x 75 JMI @ 1:10/1:15
1 x 50 kick ½ way underwater on every wall @ :40/:45
1 x 25 MAX underwater kick from Dive @ :40
1 x 100 MAX for time

    DISTANCE

4 x 200 @ :20 rest
#1 Free #2 Non-Free #3 BK/Kick by 50's #4 IM
(1:00)
12 x 50
#1-6 Neg Split (Clear/Pink) @ :45
#7-12 No Breath off walls for 3 Strokes @ :45

4 x 100 @:10 rest
#1 Free #2 Past flags on each wall choice #3 Non-Free #4 Drill
(1:00)
6 x 100
#1-3 D1-3
#4-6 Fast breakout on each wall

8 x 50 w/fins (25 underwater/25 swim) @ 1:10

2 x 400 Fin Swim
#1 Free
#2 IM

    MID-DISTANCE
1 x 300 w/fins
4 x 50 @ 1650 Pace @ 1:00

1 x Broken 200 @ 50's for :10 rest
2 x {
   4 x 100 Neg Split @ 1:30
   (White/Pink)
   4 x 50 Descend
   4 x 25 Build
   4 x 150 (breast/free/choice)
}

Thu Sep 30 2021

3 x 300 Paddle/Pull @ 3:45/4:00
BP - 5

2 x {
   3 x 50 fist drill @ 1:00
   8 x 25 #1 Stroke drill @ :45
   fly: press/pop, back: catchup, Breast: pull w/ little paddles, Free: single arm
   4 x 25 build @ :30
}
4 x 100 (50 #1 Stroke/50 Free) @ 1:30
 Stroke – easy free

IM
4 x 200 IM @ 2:45/3:00
Descend

8 x 100 IMO w/fins @ 1:20/1:30

8 x 50 @ : 45/:50
1-4 #1 Stroke, 4-8 Worst Stroke

October 2021

1 Friday
2 Saturday
3 Sunday
4 Monday
5 Tuesday
6 Wednesday
7 Thursday
8 Friday
9 Saturday
10 Sunday
11 Monday
12 Tuesday
13 Wednesday
14 Thursday
15 Friday
16 Saturday
17 Sunday
18 Monday
19 Tuesday
20 Wednesday
21 Thursday
22 Friday
23 Saturday
24 Sunday
25 Monday
26 Tuesday
27 Wednesday
28 Thursday
29 Friday
30 Saturday
31 Sunday

Fri Oct 01 2021

400 IM
8 x 50 Kick @ :10 rest
10 x 100 @ :15 rest
Odds: Back
Evens: Free

2 x 100 Paddle w/Pull Buoy @ 2:30/2:40
4 x 100 Pull @ 1:30

4 x 75 Stroke (long underwater on each wall) @ 1:20
4 x 50 25 build to top speed, 25 easy @ 1:00

    SPRINT

4 x 200 @ 2:40
1 white, 2 pink, 1 red
10 x 100 @ 1:25
4 white, 3 pink, 3 red
12 x 50 @ :50
6 pink, 6 red

1 x 200 Kick easy @ 4:00
6 x 50 kick @ 1:00
D 1-3, 4-6

    DISTANCE

5 x 500's
(white - pink - red - blue - Max for time)

    MID-DISTANCE

5 x 100 Negative Split (50 White/50 Red) @ 1:20

1 x Broken 500 @ 100's : 10 seconds

1 x 500 (200 White/300 Pink) @ 6:30/6:45
8 x 100 (alternate free/non-free) @ 1:30
1 x 300 blue @ 4:50/5:10
6 x 100 (back/free/choice/fly) @ +:10
8 x 50 Hold 1650 Goal Pace @ :50

Sat Oct 02 2021

2 x 400
#1 Free #2 IM by 100's

3 x 200
#1 RIMO #2 IM #3 Choice

3 x { w/fins
   25 underwater kick @ :30
   50 Fly descend @ :40
   75 Fast Kick - Flutter @ 1:00/1:10
   100 FAST @ 2:00
   }

2 x 400 IM JMI @ 4:30
4 x 50 Kick IMO @ :50
(1:00)
3 x 200 IM JMI @ 2:15
4 x 50 Kick IMO @ :50

Mon Oct 04 2021

400 IM
6 x 100 Kick w/Board
4 x 100 IM Order @ :15 rest

1 x 300 Kick w/ fins no board @ 4:10/4:20
4 x 50 Fast kick Flutter @ :40/:45
1 x 300 Kick w/ fins no board @ 4:00/4:10
4 x 50 Fast kick Dolphin @ :40/:45

    SPRINT

8 x 50 @ 1:00
#1-4 add up to best time 200
#5-8 Descend to MAX

10 x 25 @ :40
#1-4 MAX Breakout
#5-6 MAX Finish
#7-8 Build
#9-10 Underwater Kick

    DISTANCE

4 x 50 #1 drill, #2 build, #3 drill, #4 sprint @ :30

2 x {
1 x 100 @ 7:00
4 x 50 @ 4:00
}

1 x 400 White
10 x 100 (50 kick/50 swim) @ 1:40
8 x 50 Non-Free @ :50

    MID-DISTANCE

1 x 800 Paddle/Pull BP: 3-5-7 by 100's
8 x 100 Build to MAX last 25 @ 1:30/1:40

3 x {
  400 White @ 4:40/4:50
  2 x 100 Pink @ 1:30/1:40
  4 x 100 Red @ 1:05/1:10
  2 x 50 MAX @ 1:00
  (2:00)
}

Tue Oct 05 2021

500 Free
3 x 100 Kick w/Board
10 x 100 IM Order @ :15 rest

3 x 300 Paddle w/Pull Buoy @ 4:15
(:30)
3 x 100 Non-Free work walls @ 1:40

6 x 50 Fist Drill @ 1:00
6 x 25 Build @ :30

1 x Broken 200
1 x 100 MAX
2 x 50 MAX

Wed Oct 06 2021

3 x 200 - #1 Free #2 Non-Free #3 Choice
4 x 100 IM White

5 x 100 (Kick/Drill/Swim/Drill) @ 2:00
1 x 400 IMO w/Fins
4 x 25 underwater kick @ :30

   SPRINT

1 x 300 easy
2 x {
    100 Red from Blocks
    200 easy
    100 MAX from push
    100 easy
 }

2 x {
    50 Red from Blocks
    100 easy
    50 MAX from Push
    50 easy
 }

   DISTANCE

3 x 400 @ 4:50/5:00
Descend
4 x 50 Easy @ 1:00
3 x 300 @ 3:30/3:45
Descend
4 x 50 Easy @ 1:00
3 x 200 @ 2:20/2:30
Descend
4 x 50 Easy @ 1:00

   MID-DISTANCE

2 x 400 Paddle w/Pull Buoy @ 4:45/5:00
3 x 200 IM :30 sec
4 x 50 Free @ :40

2 x 300 (150 Free/150 Non-Free) @
4 x 100 Descend @ 1:30
4 x 50 Free @ :40

4 x 25's Max start + breakout

Thu Oct 07 2021

1 x 400 Free
1 x 300 Non-Free
1 x 200 Kick
1 x 100 IM

2 x {
1 x 300 Kick :30 sec rest
4 x 50 Kick Descend to MAX @ 1:00
}

1 x 200 Kick MAX for time @ 4:00
4 x 50 kick easy @ 1:10
1 x 100 Kick MAX for time (dolphin on back)

8 x 50 @ 1:00
1st 25: Work on MAX breakout off wall
2nd 25: Work on MAX perfect finish

2 x 200 @ 2:30/2:40
White-Pink

4 x 100 @ 1:10/1:20
Pink-Red-Blue-MAX

4 x 50 @ 1:00
odds: 25 swim/25 underwater
evens: 25 RB:0 /25 easy

4 x 100 (50 Non-Free/25 BK/25 Choice) @ 1:45

Fri Oct 08 2021

200 SKIMPS
8 x 50 IMO @ :50
300 White

4x 25 (drill/build/drill/sprint) @ :40

    SPRINT

8 x 50 (25 Drill/ 25 build to max finish) @ :50

2 x 50 MAX
6 x 25 work on breakout

4 x 50 D 1-4 @ 1:00
8 x 75 (free/kick/non-free) @ 1:20
6 x 150 (BK/free/choice) @ :10 rest

    DISTANCE

5 x 100 @ 1:20 (no breath in or out of walls) @ 1:30
8 x 50 (25 Drill/ 25 build to max finish) @ :50

4 x (300 + 100 easy)
odds: 100 Swim/100 Kick RED/100 Swim
evens: Descend each 100
(1:30)
4 x (200 + 50 easy)
#1 Pink, #2 Drop 5 secs, #3 MAX Kick, #4 Drop 3 sec from #2
(1:00)
8 x (50 + 50 easy) Descend 1-4 , hold time on 5-8

    MID-DISTANCE

2 x 800 @ 10:00/10:30
#1 -Build each 100 to Pink
#2 -Ascend each 100 starting at Pink

4 x 200 IM @ 2:40/2:50
#1-2 -(1/2 way underwater on each wall)
#3-4 -Swim

2 x 600 @ 7:30/8:00
#1 each 100 - (75 White + 25 only 2 breaths)
#2 each 100 - (50 Pink + 50 Kick no board

Sat Oct 09 2021

1 x 500 Free
1 x 400 (200 BK/200 BR)
1 x 300 Scull

2 x {
   4 x 25 fist drill
   2 x 25 Stroke build
}

3 x 200 (200 Free/200 BK/200 BR)
1 x 400 (200 Kick/100 Free/100 Choice)
1 x 400 Paddle w/Pull Buoy DPS

4 x 100 IM @ 1:35
4 x 50 Fast Kick @ 1:10
1 x 200 easy

10 x 100 MAX Kick @ 1:45

500 Cooldown

Mon Oct 11 2021

3 x 600
#1 200 RIMO/200 Swim/200 Drill
#2 300 (50 drill/50 swim best Stroke/300 kick)
#3 Swim Choice

5 x 100 @ 1:30
#1-2 Max of 2 breaths each 25
#3-4 (50 Free/50 Back)
#5 Max of 2 breaths each 25

   SPRINT

2 x (10 x 50 @ 1:30) ALL OUT MAX
Cool down

   DISTANCE

8 x 25 Sprints
1 x 300 Paddle w/Pull Buoy
10 x 100 JMI @ 1:05/1:20

2 x {
    1 x 400 Stroke
    4 x 50 @ 1:00
    Descend 1-4
}
5 x 200 @ 2:30
1-3 all White, 4-5

6 x 50 Kick MAX @ 1:00

   MID-DISTANCE

3 x 500 Max for time, from dive

Tue Oct 12 2021

600 Free
6 x 100 IM D1-3 and 4-6 @ 1:30

10 x 100 (25 drill/50 swim/25 drill) @ 1:30

3 x {
   1 x 300 – Catchup Drill
   5 x 50 drill – Choice @ 1:10
   4 x 25 Stroke @:40
}
10 x 50 w/fins 25 underwater kick/25 swim @ 1:00
4 x 25 underwater kick @ :40

5 x 100 (drill/swim) @ 1:40
2 x 200 #1 White #2 Pink @ 2:30
3 x 100 D1-3 to Pink @ 1:30
3 x 100 (drill/swim or kick/swim) @ 1:40

Wed Oct 13 2021

3 x 300
#1 Free
#2 Back
#2 (150 Kick/150 Swim choice)

4 x 100 IMO (Kick/Drill/Swim/Drill) @ 2:20
3 x 200 Free
4 x 25 kick red @ :30

     SPRINT

4 x 200 @ 2:30/2:40
(2) White-Pink-Red
4 x 100 JMI @ 1:10/1:20
(1:00)
8 x 50 Hold Goal 200 Pace + 1 @ 1:00
4 x 100 JMI @ 1:10/1:20
(2:00)
6 x 50 @ 1:00
DPS max of BR: 5 @ 1:10

     DISTANCE

5 x 100 Paddle/Pull @ 1:20/1:30
4 x (200 + 100 easy)
(2:00)
8 x (75 + 25 easy)
White-Pink-Red-White x 2
2 x (50 + 50 easy)
Hold 200 Goal Pace + 1
     MID-DISTANCE

4 x 100 IM @ 1:50 Pink

12 x 50 Fins @ :40
4 x 50 #1 drill, #2 build, #3 drill, #4 sprint @ :30

– 2 Minutes between rounds
3 x {
   200 White @ 2:40
   2 x 75 Pink @ 1:30
   4 x 50 Red @ 1:00
   2 x 25 MAX @ :40
}

Thu Oct 14 2021

1 x 500 White Kick
Non-Stop{
    400 Kick-400 Pull-400 Swim
    300 Kick-300 Pull-300 Swim
    200 Kick- 200 Pull- 200 Swim
    100 Kick- 100 Pull- 100 Swim
}

1 x 400 Build into each turn, breakout with no breath
1 x 300 Stroke

8 x 25 IM @ :40

4 x (100 IMO + 50 easy) @ 15 rest

3 x 300 @ :20 rest
5 x 100 IMO @ 1:50
#1-3: Descend
#4-6 :Descend to Max
5 x 100 JMI @ 1:10

Fri Oct 15 2021

3 x 400
#1 (200 Free/200 Back) @ :20 rest
#2 (200 Kick/200 Free) @ :20 rest
#3 (200 Choice/200 Kick no board)

8 x 50 @ 1:00
Each one work one flip turns pushing off on back
4 x 100 JMI @ 1:10/1:15
#1-2 Neg Split (White/Red)
#2-4 DPS

SPRINT

3 x 300 @ 4:00
(2) White – (1) Pink

6 x 50's MAX for time
From Dive @ 5:00

DISTANCE

5 x 200 @ 2:40
1 white, 2 pink, 2 red
12 x 100 @ 1:25
6 pink, 6 red
12 x 50 @ :50
6 Red, 6 MAX

1 x 200 Kick easy @ 4:00
4 x 50 Kick MAX @ 1:00

MID-DISTANCE

5 x 125 @ 1:50/2:00
#1-3 100 Pink + 25 Red w/2 Breaths
#4-6 100 Red + 25 MAX w/2 Breaths

6 x 150 @ 3:30 (50 Kick Blue + 100 Swim)
12 x 50 @ :50

Sat Oct 16 2021

1 x 200 Free
3 x 100 Free RB5
1 x 200 Free
3 x 100 Free RB6

2 x 300
#1 Scull
#2 (BK/Breast/Scull) by 100's

8 x 75 (Kick-Drill-Swim) @ 1:10
Sprint
3 x 200 w/fins DPS @ 2:30
    4 x 100 MAX
4 x 50 MAX
4 x 50 MAX

12 x 50 (50 Kick/50 Swim)

4 x 100 JMI

Mon Oct 18 2021

8 x 125
odds: 25 Free/50 Kick no board/50 Non-Free
evens: 50 Free/75 Kick

1 x 200 Scull on Back
1 x 200 Scull on Front

1 x 400 Kick
4 x 100 Kick (50 pink/50 red) @ 1:50
4 x 50 MAX Kick @ 1:00
1 x 200 easy

     SPRINT

8 x 100
odds: Free JMI @ 1:10/1:15
evens: Breast kick @ 1:40
(2:00)
6 x 75 D1-4 , Hold Red on 5-6 @ 1:20
4 x 50 Ascend at Blue @ 1:00

20 x 25
#1-10 w/ chutes @ :45
#11-20 w/ fins underwater kick @ :30

     DISTANCE

4 x 200 w/ fins @ 2:40/2:50
(:30)
4 x 200 IM @ 3:30
4 x 50 @ 1:30
No breath into and out of each turn
4 x 25 MAX breakout @ :30
10 x 50 MAX @ 4:00

     MID-DISTANCE

12 x 75 (2 easy @ 1:10, 1 FAST @ 1:00)

1 x 600 Pull @ 7:00/7:50
4 x 75 Kick @ 1:20
odds: White-Pink-Red
Evens: Red-Pink-White
(1:00)
1 x 600 Pull @ 6:50/7:40
4 x 100 Kick @ 1:30/1:40
Descend to MAX start @ Pink
(2:00)
2 x 500 Swim @ 5:20/5:40
(2:00)
4 x 200 Swim w/fins @ 2:15

Tue Oct 19 2021

4 x 300 Free-Kick-RIMO – (50 Swim/50 Drill)

8 x 100 @ 1:40
#1-3 (50 Kick Red/50 Kick White)
#4-7 (75 Kick Pink/25 Kick MAX)
#8 100 Kick MAX

6 x 25 @ :30
odds: MAX Breakout
evens: MAX finish

6 x (100 + 50 easy)
odds: Build each 25 to no breath in flags, fast finish
evens: max of 9 breaths

3 x 300 @ :20 rest
12 x 50 IMO @ 1:10
#1-4: Descend
#5-8: Descend
#9-12:Descend to Max
5 x 100 JMI @ 1:10

Wed Oct 20 2021

1 x 500 (250 Free/200 Non-Free/50 BK)
1 x 400 (200 Kick/200 Kick no board)
1 x 200 RIMO

2 x 200 Scull #1 Front, #2 Back
4 x 50 Fist Drill @ 1:00
4 x 75 (fist drill/swim/build) @ 1:10

SPRINT

1 x 400 Scull

1 x 400 (200 Free-White/200 Non-Free – White) @ 5:10
6 x 100 Paddle @ 1:15
#1-3 Descend, #4-6 Ascend

300 (150 Non-Free – Pink/150 Free – White) @ 4:10
4 x 100 Fins @ 1:10
1 x 200 (100 Drill/100 Kick) @ 3:10
4 x 100 JMI @ 1:10/1:20
100 Build each Turn @ 1:30
3 x 100 fast breakouts @ 1:30

DISTANCE

1 x 400 FR/Non-FR by 100
4 x 100 IM (2) White (2) Pink @ 1:45
4 x 50 JMI @ :45/:50
(2:00)
1 x 300 FR/Non-FR by 50
3 x 100 IM (2) Pink (1) Red @ 1:10
4 x 50 JMI @ :40/:45
(1:00)
1 x 200 FR/Non-FR by 100
2 x 100 JMI Red-Blue @ 1:45
4 x 50 JMI Dolphin kick @ :55/1:00

MID-DISTANCE

6 x 100 @ 1:30
1 x 400 DPS @ 5:00
8 x 50 (2 white/ 2 pink/ 2 red/ 2 pink) @ :50
(:30)
1 x 400 DPS @ 5:00
5 x 100 blue @ 1:20
(:30)
1 x 300 Negative Split @ 4:00
8 x 25 Build to MAX finish @ :30

Thu Oct 21 2021

1 x 100 SKIMPS

4 x 50 kick no board #1 stroke @ :50

6 x 200
#1-2 (100 Back/100 Breast) @ +:20 rest
#3-4 Choice Swim @ 2:40
#5-6 (50 BK/100 Kick no board/50 Choice)

2 x 100 (50FR/50 FL) @ 1:25
1 x 200 IM @ 2:45
1 x 300 FL @ 4:20 Build each 100 to great turn + great walls
1 x 200 FR White @ 2:30
1 x 300 (100BK/100BR/100FR) @ 4:30
1 x 200 FL @ 2:40
1 x 300 FR @ 3:50
1 x 400 IM @ 5:25
3 x 100 FL @ 1:35
1 x 200 FR @ 2:45

Fri Oct 22 2021

1 x 200 Kick Breast
1 x 200 Kick Fly
1 x 200 Back
1 x 200 Kick Free

6 x 100
#1-3 (Kick/Drill/Swim) @ 2:00
#4-6 Past flags on each wall @ 2:00

    SPRINT

12 x 100 IM @ 1:30

2 x {
    4 x 50 Kick @ 1:00
    1 x 200 IM @ 2:40
    1 x 300 Negative Split (150 White/150 Red) @ 5:00
}

4 x 12.5 from the Block

    DISTANCE

5 x {
    200 Best Average @ /3:20
    4 x 50 Avg. Best time 200 Pace @ 1:00
    1:00 rest
}

    MID-DISTANCE

3 x (500 + 100 easy)
#1 White
#2 Build each 100
#3 Pink

6 x (200 + 50 easy)
#1-2 IM Swim
#3-4 Kick Red
#5-6 Swim Red

10 x (100 + 50 easy)
#1-5 Hold 1000 Goal Pace +3
#6-8 Hold 1000 Goal Pace +2
#9-10 Hold 1000 Goal Pace +1

Sat Oct 23 2021

1 x 600 (300 Free-300 NonFree)
4 x 100 IMO (drill fly) @ :10 rest
8 x 50 (Fly/Free, Back/Free, Breast/Free, Free/Free) @

10 x 25 Build each 25 to fast flip @ 1:10
8 x 25 (12.5 underwater kick sprint/12.5 breakout MAX, easy) @ :30

1 x 200 Choice
6 x 50 Paddle @ :50

2 x {
1 x 200 kick White
5 x 50 Kick D 1-5
}

6 x 150 @ 2:00/2:10
#1-3 Negative Split
#4-6 Best average
(2:00)
5 x 100 JMI @ 1:00/1:05/1:10

Mon Oct 25 2021

200 SKIMPS
12 x 50 Drill IMO x 3 @ 1:00

6 x 75 (Kick/drill/swim) @ 1:10
8 x 25 @ :30
odds: drill/ evens: Stroke

    SPRINT

6 x 100 Kick @ 1:45
8 x 100 Paddle w/Pull Buoy @ :15 rest
6 x 50
odds: Red @ 1:00
evens: blue @ 1:00

200 clear
10 x 50 @ 1:30 MAX PACE

    DISTANCE

2 x 400 Paddle w/Pull Buoy @ 4:45/5:00
3 x 200 IM :30 sec
4 x 50 Free @ :40

2 x 300 (150 Free/150 Non-Free) @ 4:00
4 x 100 Descend @ 1:30
4 x 50 Free @ :40

    MID-DISTANCE

3 x 600 Paddle w/Pull Buoy
#1 Descend each 100
#2 Descend each 200
#3 Descend each 300 to MAX

8 x (150 + 50 easy)
odds: Free – Hold all same Time
evens: Non-Free Pink
8 x 50 Dolphin on Back @ 1:00

10 x (100 + 100 easy)
500 (75 Free/25 Breast)

10 x 75 (25 Kick Streamline/25 Fist/25 Build) @ 1:15

6 x 125 (25 Dolphin Kick on back/75 Back/25 underwater) @ 2:00

Tue Oct 26 2021

6 x 50 drill/swim @ 1:00
1 x 600 Paddle/Pull
Bp 5 by 100's work on great turns

10 x 100
#1-3 Free @ 1:30
#4-6 100 IM @ 1:40
#7-10 (25 No breath/50 Swim/25 1RB:1) @ 1:40
4 x 200
Free - Non Free - Kick no board - RIMO

3 x 100 (white/pink/red) @ 1:45
2 x 100 red – blue @ 1:30
4 x 50 D 1-4 @ 1:10

6 x 25 from a Dive max

4 x 200 (free/stroke/kick) @ 3:00

Wed Oct 27 2021

2 x 300
#1 Free #2 RIMO (drill fly)
6 x 50 non-free @ :15 rest
5 x 100 Paddle w/Pull Buoy @ 1:30
6 x 50 Pull @ 1:00

6 x 75 (Kick/drill/swim) @ 1:10
8 x 25 @ :30
odds: drill/ evens: stroke

    SPRINT

8 x 50 (25 Drill/ 25 build to max finish) @ :50

1 x Broken 200 @ 50
2 x 50 MAX
 Cool Down

    DISTANCE

3 x 300
#1 Free
#2 Kick/Swim by 50's
#3 Best Stroke/ Worst Stroke by 50's

4 x 100 RIMO @ 1:30
8 x 50 (Fly/Free, Back/Free, Breast/Free, Free/Free) :50
2 x {   4 x 50 w/fins kick dolphin on back @ :45
4 x 25 Build Kick w/fins @ :30
1 x 200 MAX Kick w/fins @ 4:30
}
9 x 125
#1-3 100 Build + 25 Red 2 breaths @ 1:45
#4-6 50 White + 75 Red @ 1:40
#7-9 25 MAX no breath + 75 White + 25 1 breath

    MID-DISTANCE

3 x 1000's {
    300 Pull
    500 Descend
    200 Max Kick
  }
  Men @ 12:30
  Women @ 13:30

Thu Oct 28 2021

1 x 800 (200 Free/300 Kick/200 NonFree/100 Drill)
2 x 400 #1 IM #2 Kick choice

9 x 100
#1-3 D1-3 to Pink
#4-6 Bp 5/7 by 50
#7-9 Build each turn to MAX flip + 3 MAX Strokes Breakout

IM
8 x 100 Build
#1-4 IMO w/fins @ 1:20/1:30
#5-8 IM 1:30/1:40

2 x {
    1 x 100 Back JMI @ 1:20/1:30
    4 x 25 Back 15m underwater @ :20
    1 x 100 Breast RED @ 1:45
    4 x 25 Free JMI (max of 3 breaths) @ :30
    1 x 100 Free MAX @ 4:00
}

8 x 50 Kick w/chutes IMO @ 1:20

Fri Oct 29 2021

1 x 500 Free
1 x 300 Scull

10 x 100 @ 1:30
odds: (25 kick/25 drill/50 swim with no breath turns)
evens: DPS

    SPRINT

5 x {
    100 Best Average @ 2:00
    4 x 50 Avg. Best time 200 Pace @ 1:00 + 1:00 rest
}

    DISTANCE

3 x 200 Paddle/Pull
1 x 400 easy
8 x 200 @ 2:40
#1-2 Free
#3-4 (100 Kick/100 Swim)
#5-6 Non-Free
#7-8 RIMO
15 x 100 Free @ 1:30

    MID-DISTANCE

3 x {
    1 x 200 @ 3:00 Dive
    Go 500 Pace
    2 x 100 @ 1:40 (500 pace)
    1 x 100 Dive MAX
}
10 x 50 @ 1:00
Odds 50 Kick
Evens 50 Swim

Sat Oct 30 2021

1 x 600 (200 Free/200 BK/200 Choice)
6 x 50 drill/swim @ 1:00

4 x 50 @ 1:00
9 x 100 Paddle w/Pull Buoy @ 1:30
#1-3 White
#4-6 Pink
#7-9 Red

1 x 300 Build   @ 3:15/3:30

20x 50 Blue @ :40

2 x 200 Choice @ 3:00

November 2021

1 Monday
2 Tuesday
3 Wednesday
4 Thursday
5 Friday
6 Saturday
7 Sunday
8 Monday
9 Tuesday
10 Wednesday
11 Thursday
12 Friday
13 Saturday
14 Sunday
15 Monday
16 Tuesday
17 Wednesday
18 Thursday
19 Friday
20 Saturday
21 Sunday
22 Monday
23 Tuesday
24 Wednesday
25 Thursday
26 Friday
27 Saturday
28 Sunday
29 Monday
30 Tuesday

Mon Nov 01 2021

400 IM
8 x 50 Kick @ :10 rest
10 x 100 @ :15 rest
Odds: Fly
Evens: Free

    SPRINT

4 x 100 IM @ 1:45/1:50
4 x 50 Build/MAX finish last 12.5 @ 1:00

4 x 100 IM @ 1:45/1:50
4 x 50 Build/MAX last 25 @ 1:00

4 x 100 JMI @ 1:00/1:05
(2:00)
4 x 50 @ :30/:35
10 x 50 @ 1:00
Odds 50 Kick
Evens 50 Swim

    DISTANCE
1 x 400 Free
4 x 100 IMO (optional drill fly) @ :10 rest
8 x 50 (Fly/Free, Back/Free, Breast/Free, Free/Free) @ :20
6 x 150 (drill/kick/swim) @ 2:10
6 x 50 fist drill #1 Stroke @ 1:00
4 x 25 Build

1 x 400 IM @ 5:40/6:10/6:30
4 x 50 Kick no board IMO @ :50
(2:00)
4 x 200 IM @ 3:15/3:30/3:40
8 x 50 Kick no board #1 Stroke @ :50

8 x 50 Kick Pink @ :55
4 x 50 IMO @ :50
4 x 100 Kick w/ chutes @ :30 sec rest

    MID-DISTANCE

1 x 600 Free
1 x 400 IM
8 x 50 IMO x 2 @ :10 rest
1 x 400 IM @ 5:10/5:30/6:00/6:30
4 x 50 Kick no board IMO @ :45/:50
4 x 200 IM @ 3:00/3:15/3:30/3:40
8 x 50 kick no board #1 Stroke @ :50

8 x 50 Chutes @ 1:15/1:20
10 x 50 w/ fins (12.5 underwater kick/12.5 swim) @ 1:00

Tue Nov 02 2021

4 x 200 IM
3 x 100 Freestyle
1 x 200 Kick

2 x {
   8 x 50 Kick #1 Stroke D1-4 , 5-8 to MAX
   1 x 400 Kick no board
}

8 x 50 @ 1:00
#1-4 Descend 1-4
#5-8 DPS

2 x (10 x 50 KICK @ 1:30) ALL OUT MAX

400 Free @
4 x 100 (50 Kick/50 Swim) @ 1:40

Wed Nov 03 2021

4 x 200
IM-NonFree-Free-Kick

4 x 75 (25 fist drill/25 swim/25 build) @ 1:20
8 x 50 (25 kick no board/25 swim) @ 1:00

  SPRINT

4 x 100 feet past flags on every wall @ 1:30
8 x 25 Sprints @ :30

2 x 400 #1 Free #2Back/Breast by 50's
4 x 125 Paddle/fins working on awesome catch @ 1:30
(1:00)
300 Non Free
4 x 100 @ 1:20/1:30 MAX
300 Cooldown

  DISTANCE

4 x (200 + 100 easy)
D 1-4
4 x (75 + 25 easy)
All Red
8 x (50 + 50 easy)
D 1-4 , D 5-8 to MAX

  MID-DISTANCE

10 x (50 + 50 easy)
Hold 500 Goal Pace - 1
(2:00)

3 x 300 + 100 easy (300 - Neg Split)
200 + 100 easy (200 - out pace of 1000)
100 + 50 easy (100 - out pace of 500)
50 + 50 easy (50 - MAX)

1 x 800 Fin Swim
(1:00)
5 x 100 w/fins @ 1:20/1:35
add up to best time 500

Thu Nov 04 2021

1 x 300 Free
2 x 100 BackStroke
1 x 200 Free
2 x 100 Back

10 x 50 (Kick/Drill) @ :55
1 x 400 Paddle/Fins
4 x 25 sprint kick @ :50

9 x 100 w/fins @ 1:20/1:30
4 x 150 Paddles/Fins @ 1:45/1:50

IM
2 x 300 (75 IMO) @ 4:10/4:15
4 x 150 (50 BK/100 Breast) @ 2:15/2:20
4 x 150 (50 BR/100 Free) @ 2:05/2:10

Fri Nov 05 2021

1 x 400 IM
1 x 200 Kick with board
2 x 100 Freestyle

1 x 300 (150 Kick no board/ 150 Swim) @ 5:30
1 x 500 white
2 x 300 Pull @ 3:45/4:00
10 x 50 @ 1:00
Odds 50 Free
Evens 50 Non Free

    SPRINT

15 x 100
#1-3 Free @ 1:30
#4-6 Build each 50 to MAX flip @ 1:30
#7-9 Kick @ 2:00
#10-12 (50 BK/50 Scull) @ 1:50
#13-15 D1-3 to Pink @ 1:30

400 Kick
4 x 50 Kick Descend

    DISTANCE

5 x {
   300 Best Average @ 3:50
   3 x 100 Goal 500 Pace @ 1:30
   1:00 rest
   }

    MID-DISTANCE

5 x 200 2 white, 2 pink, 1 red@ 2:40
(1:00)
8 x 150 2 white, 2 pink, 2 red, 2 blue@ 2:00
(1:00)
10 x 100 2 white, 2 pink, 2 red, 2 blue 2 MAX@ 1:45

Cooldown – 4 x 100 choice @ 1:40

Sat Nov 06 2021

1 x 400 IM
4 x 200 IM @ 2:50
9 x 100 @ 1:15 BP: 3-5

2 x {
   4 x 50 Fist Drill @ 1:10
   2 x 25 Build to Pink @ :30
}

1 x 500 White
5 x 100 @ 1:05/1:10/1:15

1 x 400 White
4 x 100 @ 1:05/1:10/1:15

1 x 300 White
3 x 100 @ 1:05/1:10/1:15

1 x 200 White
2 x 100 @ 1:05/1:10/1:15

Mon Nov 08 2021

4 x 200 Paddle w/Pull Buoy @ 2:20/2:30/2:40

10 x 25 Build each 25 to fast flip @ :50
8 x 25 (12.5 underwater kick sprint/12.5 breakout MAX, easy) @ :30

    SPRINT

6 x 50 @ 5:00
#1-2 MAX 2 Breaths TOTAL
#3-4 MAX 1 Breath TOTAL
#5-6 MAX 0 Breath TOTAL

4 x 50 MAX w/ fins from dive
1 x 50 w/ fins from push

    DISTANCE

8 x 50 (25 Drill/ 25 build to max finish) @ :50

1 x Broken 200 @ 50
2 x Broken 100 @ 50 & 75

5 x 100 Kick @ 1:45
2 x 100 Pull @ 1:20

    MID-DISTANCE

4 x 200 @ 2:20/2:30
Build each 100 to Pink – no breath from flags to wall on finish

Tue Nov 09 2021

2 x 300 DPS @ 4:00
5 x 100 (3) White (2) Pink @ 1:30

10 x 50 Kick @ :55
1 x 400 IM w/Fins
4 x 25 sprint kick @ :50

4 x 200
odds: Free @ 2:20/2:30
evens: Stroke 2:30/2:40/2:50
8 x 50
odds: Free RB:2 @ :45
evens: non-free @ 1:00

300 (100 BK/100 Choice/100 breast)

Wed Nov 10 2021

2 x 200
#1 Kick Choice
#2 Kick no Board
200 IM

3 x 600 @ + :15 rest
#1 Paddle/Pull
#2 Paddle
#3 Descend each 100 to Pink

SPRINT

5 x 100 Kick w/fins @ 1:15
4 x 200 Paddle w/Pull Buoy
6 x 50
odds: Red @ 1:00
evens: Easy @ 1:00

200 clear
10 x 50 @ 1:30 MAX PACE

DISTANCE

8 x 100 (Kick/Drill) Worst Stroke @ 1:45
1 x 500 Paddle/Pull
6 x 100 IM @ 1:30/1:40
1 x 500 Free @ 6:20

8 x 75
odds: Fly @ 1:20
evens: Free DPS @ 1:15

12 x 100
#1-4 @ 1:30
#5-8 @ 1:20
#9-10 @ 1:15
#11-12 @ 1:10

MID-DISTANCE

3 x 200 IM @ 3:00/3:10
3 x 200 (Kick no Board/Kick board /Choice)
(1:00)
4 x 25 underwater kick @ :45
4 x 25 underwater with arms @ :40
4 x 25 (1/2 way underwater MAX kick + breakout/easy) @ :30
(1:00)
3 x 200 IM :30 sec
6 x 100 JMI @ 1:05/1:10/1:15
(1:00)
2 x 100 JMI @ 1:00/1:05/1:10

Thu Nov 11 2021

500 Free
200 Back

3 x200
#1 Free
#2 (Back/Breast by 50's)
#3 (100 Choice/100 IM)

6 x 100 DPS @ :50

8 x 100 (25 easy/50 RB: 5 /25 Pink) @ 1:30

3 x {
   1 x 75 MAX + :30 rest + 50 MAX from push
}

2 x {
   1 x 50 MAX + :30 rest + 25 MAX from push
}

Fri Nov 12 2021

400 RIMO

6 x 100 Non-Free (50 Kick/50 Swim) @ :10 rest
12 x 50 (4 x Fly/Free, Back/Free, Breast/Free) @ :10 rest

8 x 50 (25 Drill/ 25 build to max finish) @ :50
5 x 100 Stroke @ 1:10/1:20/1:30/1:40

    SPRINT

3 x 200 @ 3:00
IM – Choice – RIMO
4 x 100 @ 1:25
(2) Clear – (2) White
3 x 300 @ 4:20
Kick – Free – IM
6 x 100 @ 1:25
(3) White – (3) Pink

    DISTANCE

4 x 200
odds: Free @ 2:30/2:40
evens: IM @ 2:30/2:40

8 x (100 IM + 25 easy) @ 2:00/2:15
(2:00)
8 x (50 + 25 easy) @ 1:10/1:20/1:30
odds: Fly-Back-Breast Descend
evens: IMO Red

8 x 50 Stroke
#1-4 @ :40/:45
#5-8 Red @ :35/:40

    MID-DISTANCE

6 x 75
odds: Fast @ 1:10
evens: Easy @ 1:20
5 x 100 Kick w/fins @ 1:10
200 Cooldown
2 x (10 x 50 @ 1:30) ALL MAX

Sat Nov 13 2021

1 x 300 Free
2 x 200 (100 Kick/100 Swim Non-Free)

8 x 50 IMO @ :50

6 x 150 Fins/ @ 1:30

1 x 600 Kick @ 11:00
6 x 50 Kick D1-6 @ 1:00
1 x 100 MAX Kick

Fly
5 x 100 Neg Split @ 1:30
5 x (200 @ 2:40/2:50 + 3 x 100 @ 1:30)
4 x 50 MAX kick dolphin on back @ 1:00

Mon Nov 15 2021

1 x 800 Free RB4
1 x 100 Kick

6 x 100 Paddle w/Pull Buoy @ 1:20/1:30

6 x 75 Descend @ 1:10
odds: fly-back-breast
evens: back-breast-free

SPRINT

6 x 50 @ 4:00
#1-2 MAX 2 Breaths TOTAL
#3-4 MAX 1 Breath TOTAL
#5-6 MAX 0 Breath TOTAL

4 x 25 MAX w/ fins from dive
1 x 50 w/ fins from push

DISTANCE

6 x 100 (white/pink/red/blue) @ 1:25

8 x 25 from a dive w/ 5 Strokes fast @ 1:00 rest

1 x 100 Broken @ the 50 and the 75 @ 4:00 rest
2 x 50 MAX from a dive @ 3:00 rest
4 x 25's Max start + breakout, easy finish

1 x 500 White @ 6:30/7:00
4 x 100 Kick D 1-4 @ 1:50
5 x 50 (25 kick BR/25 swim choice) @ 1:00

MID-DISTANCE

8 x 100 IM @ 1:20/1:30
4 x 100 FL or FR Build to no breath/RED finish @ 1:20/1:30
4 x 50 Best Average @ :40/:50
4 x 200 IM @ 2:30/2:40
4 x 100 FL or FR Build max of 5 breaths last 50 @ 1:20/1:30
4 x 50 Best Average @ :40/:50
4 x 100 JMI @ 1:00/1:05
(2:00)
4 x 50 @ :30/:35
10 x 50 @ 1:00
Odds 50 Kick
Evens 50 Swim

Tue Nov 16 2021

8 x 100 @ 1:30
odds: Free
evens: (50 Fly drill/50 Choice)

1 x 400 (200 Kick/100 Free/100 Drill)
8x 100 paddle/pull @ 1:40/1:50
BP 5 by 100's
4 x 100 Paddle w/fast legs @ 1:10/1:20

IM
8 x (50 + 50 easy)
Hold 200 Goal Pace
(2:00)
2 x {
   200 + 100 easy (200 - Neg Split)
   100 + 50 easy (100 - out pace of 200 + 6
   2 x (50 + 50 easy) (50 - Last 100 Split of 200 divided by 2)
}
1 x 400 Fin Swim
(1:00)
2 x (100 w/fins + 100 easy)
add up to best time 200

Wed Nov 17 2021

500 Free
200 Back

3 x200
#1 Free
#2 (Back/Breast by 50's)
#3 (100 Choice/100 IM)

4 x 50 choice @ 1:10

4 x 50 choice @ 1:10

3 x 300 (100 Moderate/100 Drill/100 Build to Pink) @ 3:50/4:00/4:10
4 x 100 Negative Split (50 White/50 Red) @ 1:10/1:20
4 x 50 @ :40

    SPRINT @ 3:00

5 x 100 MAX

    DISTANCE

3 x 200 @ 2:20/2:30
8 x (100 Fast + 50 easy)
4 x (50 MAX + 50 easy)

    MID-DISTANCE

2 x Broken 500
200 (White/Pink) @ :10 rest
100 Red @ :10 rest
100 Blue @ 10 rest
100 MAX
Take overall time -:30

1 x Broken 1650
300 (Build) @ :10
200 White @ :10 rest
5 x 100 Best Avg @ :10 rest
300 (150 Pink – 150 Red) :10
150 MAX

Thu Nov 18 2021

100 SKIMPS
3 x 100 IM – Choice – Non Free
4 x 100 @ 1:25
8 x 50 @ 1:00

4 x 75
Each 25 - 12.5 underwater kick/12.5 swim
4 x 25 underwater Kick @ :40

2 x 500 Paddle/Fins @ 6:00/6:30
#1 Build each 100 to MAX flip + 5 Strokes MAX no breath
#2 Descend 100's

3 x 500 @ 7:30/7:50
Bp 3-5-7-5-3 by 100's

4 x 400 Paddle/Pull D 1-4 @ 5:20

6 x 150 (FL/BK/BR) w/ fins @ 2:10

6 x 150 @ 2:00
D 1-3, 4-6 to MAX

Fri Nov 19 2021

400 RIMO
6 x 100 Non-Free (50 Kick/50 Swim) @ :10 rest

10 x 50 @:50
Split by 25s
odds: RB 1 breath/ RB 2

    SPRINT

6 x 100 Stroke@ 1:30
Odds: Work Turns
Evens: Work Finish

1 x 400 (200 White/200 Pink) + 100 easy
4 x (200 + 100 easy)
D 1-4
8 x (100 + 50 easy)
D 1-4 , Hold 5-8
8 x (50 MAX + 50 easy)

    DISTANCE

4 x 100 MAX KICK @ 1:40
400 Easy
5 x 75 MAX @ 5:00
400 Easy
4 x 100 MAX Kick @ 1:40
4 x 50 MAX @ 3:00

    MID-DISTANCE

2 x 300 Paddle/ @ 3:30/3:40/3:50
(1)White – (1)Descend to Pink

4 x 50 IMO (Drill Fly) @ 1:10
2 x 300 (100 Free/100 BK/100 Breast) @
4 x 50 RIMO (Drill Fly) @ 1:10
6 x 75 @ 1:20
odds: Free/Non-Free/BK
evens: BK/choice/free

Sat Nov 20 2021

1 x 200 Kick no board
1 x 200 Kick w/Board
1 x 200 Kick w/ fins
1 x Kick on Back

6 x 50 Kick @ 1:00
1 x 300 easy kick
8 x 50 Kick w/fins @ :30/:35

8 x 25 Fist @ :30
4 x 25 Build @ :30
4 x 25 MAX @ :30

2 x 400 IM@ 4:50/5:10
(1:00)
2 x 200 IM @ 2:20/2:30
Pink-Red

10 x 100 IM
odds: Blue @ 1:30
evens: Pink @ 1:45

12 x 50 all FAST @ 1:00

Mon Nov 22 2021

1 x 400 Free
1 x 300 Non-Free
2 x 200 Kick
4 x 100 IM (drill fly)
8 x 50 w/chutes @ 1:10
odds: (25 no breath/25 Pink)
evens: (25 Pink/25 Red)
6 x 25 Build @ :30

10 x 25 w/ chutes @ :45 Red
10 x 25 x/ fins MAX underwater kick @ :30
2 x {
   4 x 200 @ 2:30
   (1:00)
}

    SPRINT

8 x 25 Kick w/chutes @ :45
8 x 25 Swim MAX w/fins @ :40

4 x 200{
   #1 8 x 25 @ :25 max of 2 breaths
   #2 2 x 100 @ 1:25 (1 Red, 1 Blue)
   #3 4 x 50 Kick (1 Red/1 White) @ :55
   #4 200 Negative Split
}
8 x 50 w/chutes @ 1:20
#1-4 D1-4 , #4-8 Kick D1-4 to Max

    DISTANCE

8 x 50 (25 Drill/ 25 build to max finish) @ :50
6 x 75 @ 5:00 MAX
4 x 50 @ 4:00 MAX
1 x 400 (Non-Free/Choice/BK/Choice)

    MID-DISTANCE

6 x 100 @ 1:30
1 x 400 DPS @ 5:00
8 x 50 (2 white/ 2 pink/ 2 red/ 2 pink) @ :50
(:30)
1 x 400 DPS @ 5:00
5 x 100 blue @ 1:20
(:30)
1 x 300 Negative Split @ 4:00
8 x 25 Build to MAX finish @ :30

Tue Nov 23 2021

3 x 300
#1 White/Pink @ 3:50/3:55
#2 (50 Pink/50 max of 4 breaths) @ 4:00
#3 No Breath in or out of walls

3 x 400
#1 Paddle w/Pull Buoy @ 5:00/5:10/5:20
#2 Swim BP: 3,5 by 100 @ 4:40/4:50/5:00
#3 Swim (75 Free/25 Back w/1/2 underwater kick)

5x 200 @ :10(100 Pink/50 Build /50 White)

10 x 100 JMI
#1-5 @ 1:10/1:15
#6-10 @ 1:05/1:10
(2:00)
8 x 50 @ :35/:40

Wed Nov 24 2021

500 SKIMPS
4 x 100 IM @ 1:20/1:40

1 x 400 (100 Free/100 Non-Free/100 Kick no board/100 Free/100 Non Free)
8 x 75 (Free/Non-Free/Drill) @ 1:10

1 x 400 Kick

SPRINT

5 x 75 Red @ 3:00
6 x 50 Blue@ 2:00

400 IM
4 x 100 @ 1:30
odds: Free evens: Non-free
5 x 50 drill @ 1:00
8 x 50 @ 1:00

DISTANCE

8 x 200 2 white, 2 pink, 2 red, 2 blue@ 2:30/2:40
(1:00)

9 x 100 3 white, 3 pink, 3 red @ 1:20/1:30
(1:00)
4 x 100 (50 Red/50 White) @ 1:50
Cooldown – 4 x 100 choice @ 1:40

MID-DISTANCE

1 x 600 Paddle/Pull
Bp 3-5 by 100's
1 x 400 Build

10 x 100 JMI @ 1:10/1:15
Keep all the same speed

3 x (100 + 100 easy)
Hold 1000 Pace

Thu Nov 25 2021

500 Free
6 x 100 IM @ :15 rest
4 x 100 Kick IM Order

2 x {
   100 Drill #1 Stroke @ 1:50
   2 x 75 (White/Pink/Blue) @ 1:10
   2 x 50 @ :35/:450
   2 x 25 underwater kick @ :30
}
4 x 150 Kick (White/Pink/Build to MAX finish) @ 2:15

Free
12 x 100
odds: RB5 @ 1:40
evens: RB6 @ 1:30
2 x 800 @ :30 rest
#1 Negative Split #2 Ascend
8 x 100 JMI @ 1:05/1:10

Fri Nov 26 2021

1000 Choice white
10 x 50 Kick D 1-4, 5-10 White
2 x {
   4 x 50 Catchup @ 1:10
   }

    SPRINT
1 x 400 (FR/Non-FR by 100)
4 x 100 (2) White (2) Pink @ 1:45
4 x 50 Worst Stroke @ 1:20
1 x 300 (50 BK/50 BR)
3 x 100 (2) Pink (1) Red @ 1:45
3 x 50 (25 underwater/25 easy) @ 1:35
1 x 200 (FR/Non-FR by 100)
2 x 100 (1) Red (1) Blue @ 1:45
2 x 50 Best Stroke Drill @ 1:20
8 x 50 Kick MAX @ 1:10

    DISTANCE

6 x 25 @ :30
odds: MAX Breakout
evens: MAX finish

6 x (100 + 50 easy)
odds: Build each 25 to no breath in flags, fast finish
evens: max of 9 breaths

3 x 300 @ + :20
#1: Free-NonFree-Fee by 100
#2 BP: 3-5-3 by 100
#3 BP: 5-7 by 50

12 x 50 Choice @ 1:10
#1-4: Descend
#5-8: Descend
#9-12:Descend to Max
5 x 100 JMI @ 1:10/1:15/1:20

    MID-DISTANCE

1 x 1650 Broken
200 White @ :10 rest
300 (150 Pink-150 Red) @ :10 rest
200 Red @ :10 rest
300 (Build to Blue) @ :10 rest
5 x 100 Best Avg @ :10 rest
150 MAX
Take total time – 1:30

3 x 200 MAX @ 6:00

Sat Nov 27 2021

1 x 300 Free
2 x 200 #1 Kick no board, #2 Kick Board
5 x 100 odds: IM, evens: Choice

2 x {
   4 x 50 fist drill @ 1:00
   4 x 25 build @ :30
}
8 x 50 Kick @ 1:00
D1-4 , 5-8 to MAX (start at Pink)

5 x 100 @ 1:40
odds: Build each 25 to MAX flip
evens: Build each 25 to MAX finish

1 x 400 @ 4:50/5:10
4 x 100 @ 1:10/1:20
Negative Split (White/Red)

1 x 800 @ 9:30/10:15
4 x 200 @ 2:30/2:40
(2) White (2) Pink

6 x 50 @ 1:00
odds: 25 underwater/25 swim
evens: 25 swim no breath/25 choice

4 x 100 (50 Non-Free/25 BK/25 Choice) @ 1:45

Mon Nov 29 2021

4 x 200
#1 White/Pink @ :20 rest
#2 IM order @ :30 rest
#3 Freestyle @ :10 rest
#4 No Breath in or out of walls

3 x 300 @ 3:45/3:55
(1:00)
8 x 25 Paddles DPS – Count Stroke per 25 @ :45
4 x 25 Keep Same Stroke Count as w/ paddles per 25

5 x 50 drill @ 1:00

4 x 25 Kick Build each 25 @ :40
4 x 50 Kick Descend @ :55
4 x 25 Kick @ :30

9 x 50 (2 @ :40, 1 @ :30)

    SPRINT

1 x 500
odd 100's: Free
even 100's: Build Kick

5 x 200 @ 2:40
D1-5
(2:00)
12 x 50 JMI @ :35/:45
2 x 300 (150 White/Build) @ 4:00

    DISTANCE

3 x 200 @ 2:50
3 x 400 Clear-White-Pink 5:50
3 x 300 White-Pink-Red   4:50
3 x 200 Pink-Red-Blue   3:50
3 x 100 Red-Blue-MAX   1:30

    MID-DISTANCE

3 x 500 Best Time + 30 @ 5:30/6:00/6:20
(2:00)
8 x 200 Best Average @ 2:20/2:30
(2:00)

Tue Nov 30 2021

1 x 200 Kick no board
3 x 100 Back Stroke
1 x 200 Kick with board
3 x 100 Freestyle

1000 Kick w/Board
2 x 200 IMO

3 x 400 w/fins BP: 3,5 by 100s @ 5:10
3 x 100 w/fins @ 1:15

2 x {
    3 x 200 Paddle w/Pull Buoy
    6 x 100 @ 1:05/1:10
}

December 2021

1 Wednesday
2 Thursday
3 Friday
4 Saturday
5 Sunday
6 Monday
7 Tuesday
8 Wednesday
9 Thursday
10 Friday
11 Saturday
12 Sunday
13 Monday
14 Tuesday
15 Wednesday
16 Thursday
17 Friday
18 Saturday
19 Sunday
20 Monday
21 Tuesday
22 Wednesday
23 Thursday
24 Friday
25 Saturday
26 Sunday
27 Monday
28 Tuesday
29 Wednesday
30 Thursday
31 Friday

Wed Dec 01 2021

1 x 500 (200 Free/200 Non-Free/100 RIMO)
8 x 100 @ :10 rest
odds: # 1 Stroke (50 drill/50 swim)
evens: (50 Bk/50 BR)

10 x 50 Back Drill @ :55
2 x 200 Paddles
4 x 50 kick @ :50

    SPRINT

3 x 200 Best Average @ 3:00/3:10
4 x 50 Avg. Best time @ 1:00

2 x 50's max for time

    DISTANCE

8 x 100 IM @ 1:20/1:30
4 x 75 FL or FR Build/MAX finish last 12.5 @ 1:00
4 x 25 MAX kick to 15m @ :30

4 x 200 IM @ 2:35/2:40
4 x 50 FR or FL Build/MAX last 25 @ 1:00
4 x 25 MAX kick to 15m @ :25

4 x 100 JMI @ 1:00/1:05
(2:00)
4 x 50 @ :30/:35

10 x 50 @ 1:00
Odds 50 Kick
Evens 50 Swim

    MID-DISTANCE

10 x 75 @ 1:10
#1-5 (easy/medium/fast kick slow arms)
#6-10 IMO + free

4 x (200 pad/pull + 100 easy)
Descend
5 x (100 + 50 easy)
#1-5 Goal 500 Pace

4 x (50 + 50 easy) All FAST

Thu Dec 02 2021

1 x 400 (200 Free/200 Back)
1 x 300 (150 Kick non-free/150 kick breast)
1 x 200 (100 BK/100 Choice)
1 x 100 IM

8 x 75 @ 1:30
odds: Free drill
evens: Non-Free drill

2 x 8 x 50 (25 Drill/ 25 build to max finish) @ :50
6 x 100 Kick w/fins @ 1:20/1:30
25 underwater kick/25 dolphin on back/50 kick choice

12 x 25 @ :30
underwater kick w/fins
(1:00)
4 x 50 Dolphin on back w/fins @ :45
(:30)
4 x 50 Dolphin on back w/fins @ :40

1 x 400 Free @ 4:50
2 x 50 Hold Goal 200 Pace @ 1:00
1 x 400 Free @ 5:00
2 x 50 Hold Goal 200 Pace @ 1:00
1 x 400 Free @ 5:10
2 x 50 Hold Goal 200 Pace @ 1:00

Fri Dec 03 2021

400 Kick
8 x 100 Choice @ :15 rest
2 x {
   6 x 50 Kick w/fins @ :40
   4 x 25 Underwater w/fins @ :30
   (1:00)
}

    SPRINT

4 x 200 DPS @ 3:50
4 x 50 Non-Free @ :55

4 x 200 IM @ 3:00
5 x 100 IM @ 1:30

8 x 100 @ 1:40
  odds: Red Choice
  evens: 50 RB: 4/50 easy

4 x 25's Max start + breakout, easy finish

    DISTANCE

1 x 400 easy Kick
8 x 50 Kick
#1-4 Descend to Pink
#5-8 Dolphin on back all Red

4 x 300 DPS @ 3:40/3:50/4:00
8 x 50 Non-Free @ :50

4 x 200 IM @ 2:30/2:40/2:50

8 x (50 IMO + choice 50) @ 1:30
Pink IMO
8 x 100 @ 1:40
odds: 50 kick/50 swim
evens: 50 swim max of 5 breaths
    MID-DISTANCE

8 x 100 IM pink @ 1:50

1 x Broken 1650
1 x 500 Build @ :10 rest
1 x 500 D 100's 1-5 @ :15 rest
1 x 500 Red @ :20 rest
1 x 100 Blue @ :10 rest
1 x 50 MAX

1 x 800 White @ :20 rest
4 x 50 Kick @ 1:00

Sat Dec 04 2021

1 x 300 Free
1 x 200 Non-Free
1 x 100 Kick
4 x 50 IMO @ :10 rest
6 x 150 w/fins @ :10
odd: kick-swim-kick
even: swim-kick-swim

1 x 400 Kick White @ 7:00
1 x 200 Drill

8 x 50 (25 Drill/ 25 build to max finish) @ :50

2 x 200 @ 2:40
4 x 50 Non-Free @ :50
3 x 100 @ 1:20
4 x 50 kick no board @ 1:00
1 x 200 Kick Pink @ 4:00
4 x 50 D 1-4 @ 1:00

8 x 25 Breakout

Mon Dec 06 2021

1 x 600 Free
1 x 400 IM
1 x 200 Back
1 x 500 Kick
4 x 100 Kick (50 easy/50 Red) @ 2:00

1 x 300 Scull
4 x 50 Dolphin on Back @ :50

4 x 100 (Kick/Drill) Worst Stroke @ 1:50
1 x 700 Paddle/Pull

    SPRINT

6 x 100 w/fins (25 kick/50 swim/25 dolphin on back) @ 1:40

2 x 300 White @ 4:00
4 x 50 D 1-4 @ 1:00
2 x 200 White @ 2:40
4 x 50 D 1-4 @ 1:00
2 x 100 White @ 1:35
4 x 50 Max Breakout @ 1:35

    DISTANCE

 3 x (500 + 100 easy)
#1 Paddle/Pull - White
#2 Paddle - Pink
#3 Swim - Red

3 x (300 + 100 easy)
White-Pink-(2) Red
(1:00)
1 x (200 MAX + 100 easy)
3 x (200 + 100 easy)
Pink-Red-Blue
(1:00)
1 x (100 MAX + 100 easy)

2 x (100 + 50 easy)
Pink-Red
1 x (50 MAX + 50 easy)

    MID-DISTANCE

1 x 800 White
4 x 200 descend each 200 @ 2:40
(2:00)
8 x 100 JMI @ 1:10/1:15
4 x 100 @ 1:35
(1:00)
4 x 75 Build @ 1:00

Tue Dec 07 2021

1 x 400 IM
3 x 100 Freestyle
2 x 200 IM

2 x {
   x 50 fist drill @ 1:00
   6 x 25 Build @ :30
}

8 x 75 w/fins @ :55
Continuous IM (BR-dolphin kick), Work under waters - easy swim
(:30)
4 x 50 IMO @ :50
25 underwater/25 swim
(1:00)

  4 x {
    4 x 25 fly max
    6 x 50 back red
    4 x 75 breast blue
    1 x 100 free max
  }

Wed Dec 08 2021

1 x 500 (200 Free/200 Non-Free/100 RIMO)
8 x 100 @ :10 rest
odds: #1 Stroke (50 drill/50 swim)
evens: (50 Bk/50 BR)

3 x 400
#1 Paddle w/Pull Buoy @ 5:00/5:10/5:20
#2 Swim BP: 3,5 by 100 @ 4:40/4:50/5:00
#3 Swim (75 Free/25 Back w/1/2 underwater kick)

    SPRINT

3 x 200 1 white, 1 pink, 1 red @ 2:40

8 x 100 4 white, 2 pink, 2 red @ 1:20
4 x 50 Goal 200 Pace @ 1:00
8 x 100 (50 Blue/50 choice) @ 2:00

Cooldown – 4 x 100 choice @ 1:40
    DISTANCE

5 x 100 @ 1:30

1 x 400 DPS @ 5:20
8 x 50 (2 white/ 2 pink/ 2 red/ 2 pink) @ :50
(:30)
1 x 400 pull @ 5:00
3 x 100 (2) White (1) Pink
(:30)
1 x 400 pull @ 5:00
5 x 100 blue @ 1:20

    MID-DISTANCE

2 x 600 @ 7:40/7:50
Odd 200s - DPS
8 x 100 D 1-6 , Hold time on 7-8 @ 1:30
(2:00)
6 x 75 w/chutes @ 1:20
D1-3, 4-6

2 x 400 @ 5:00/5:10
4 x 100 JMI @ 1:05/1:10
(1:00)
8 x 50 Hold 500 Goal Pace or 200 Goal Pace + 2 @ 1:00

Thu Dec 09 2021

1 x 500 (250 Free/250 Back)
1 x 100 Scull on back, arms at side
1 x 100 Scull on front, arms at side

5 x 50 @ 1:00
5 x 50 drill same Stroke different drill @ 1:00

12 x 50 Paddle/Pull @ :45

IM
3 x (200 + 50 easy) build 4th 25 to MAX transition turn + 5 Strokes breakout
#1 (100 Fly/100 Back)
#2 (100 Back/100 Breast)
#3 (100 Breast/100 Free)

4 x (75 IMO Pink + 50 Red next Stroke)

4 x (25 Blue IMO w/ blue transition turn + 50 pink)
ex. Round 1 - 25 blue fly + 50 pink back work transition turn and breakout

6 x 50 (25 kick MAX Dolphin underwater/25 swim) w/fins

Fri Dec 10 2021

4 x 100 Freestyle
3 x 100 Fly
2 x 100 Back
1 x 100 Breast

5 x 200 :20
#1 Kick
#2 Paddle w/Pull Buoy White
#3 Paddle w/Pull Buoy Pink
#4 Paddle w/Pull Buoy Red
#5 Kick

    SPRINT

3 x 200 w/fins DPS @ 2:30

8 x 200 @ 2:40
#1 (25 Red + 175 White)
#2 (50 Red + 150 White)
#3 (75 Red + 125 White)
#4 (100 Red + 100 White)
#5 (125 Blue + 75 White)
#6 (150 Blue + 50 White)
#7 (175 Blue + 25 White)
#8 200 MAX

1 x 400 (50 Free/50 Non-Free)
8 x 50 KICK D1-4, 5-8 to MAX @ 1:00

    DISTANCE

2 x 200 Broken @ :50
6 x 50 Red @ 1:00

1 x 500 Free

2 x 200 @ :20 rest
#1 Choice
#2 Non-Free

    MID-DISTANCE

1 x 500 MAX
3 x 200 MAX

Sat Dec 11 2021

200 SKIMPS
1 x 500 Kick

2 x 100 Paddle w/Pull Buoy @ 2:30/2:40
4 x 100 Pull @ 1:30

4 x 75 Stroke (long underwater on each wall) @ 1:20
4 x 50 25 build to top speed, 25 easy @ 1:00

IM
8 x 200 IMO @ :30 rest
2 x 200 IM @ 2:50
Pink-Red
(2:00)
4 x 200 @ :20 rest
#1 IM (50 drill/50 swim Pink)
#2 RIMO (50 Kick Red no board/50 Swim)
4 x 100 IMO @ 1:30
Pink-Red-Blue-MAX

Mon Dec 13 2021

1 x 500 Free RB5
3 x 100 Kick
3 x 100 Free RB5

10 x 100 @ 1:30
odds: (25 kick/25 drill/50 swim with no breath turns)
evens: DPS

SPRINT

400 Free
200 Kick
100 IM

8 x 25 MAX on 1:00
10 x 25 w/ chutes @ :45 Red
10 x 25 x/ fins MAX underwater kick @ :30

DISTANCE

3 x {
   1 x (300 + 100 easy)
   4 x (50 + 50 MAX)
}
4 x 50 MAX Kick no board @ 1:00

MID-DISTANCE

4 x 200
Pull - Kick - Pink - White
2 x 800
odd 100's: Descend
even 100's Kick Pink
6 x 200
odds: Blue @ 2:20
evens: IM @ 2:40
5 x 100's
(100's Descend 1-5 Red + 25 MAX)

Tue Dec 14 2021

3 x 500
#1 IM
#2 IM
#3 Choice Swim

6 x 50 Fist Drill @ 1:006 x 25 Build to great finish @ :30

2 x {
    1 x 300 Kick (150 White w/board/150 Pink no board) @ 5:45
    4 x 50 Descend to MAX @ 1:00
    4 x 25 Dolphin on back @ :30
}

3 x 300 Kick w/fins @ 3:45/4:00/4:10

1 x 800 Paddle/Pull @ :20 rest
4 x 200 @ 2:50/3:00
White-Pink-Red-Blue

8 x 200 @ 2:20/2:30
#1 25 Blue/175 easy
#2 50 Blue/150 easy
etc..

Wed Dec 15 2021

1 x 200 Back Stroke
1 x 200 Fly
1 x 200 Free
1 x 200 Breast
1 x 200 kick

1 x 300 Kick w/ fins no board @ 4:10/4:20
4 x 50 Fast kick Flutter @ :40/:45
1 x 300 Kick w/ fins no board @ 4:00/4:10
4 x 50 Fast kick Dolphin @ :40/:45

SPRINT

6 x 100 (white-pink-red-blue) @ 1:15

4 x 25 Fast @ 1:00 rest

2 x 100 Broken @ the 50 and the 75 @ 4:00 rest
2 x 50 MAX from a dive @ 2:30 rest
2 x 25 MAX

DISTANCE

1 x 50 MAX from Dive @ :30
1 x 200 JMI @ 2:05
1 x 25 MAX underwater kick from Dive @ :40
1 x 200 MAX for time

MID-DISTANCE

2 x 800 (400 White/400 Red) @ :30 sec rest
(1:00)
4 x (200 + 50 easy)
odds: Pink
evens: Max Turns
(1:00)
8 x (100 + 50 easy)
D1-4 , Hold #4 time on 5-8

Thu Dec 16 2021

4 x 200 @ :15 rest
odds: Free
evens: (50 breast drill/50 Choice)

3 x 100 Non-Free work walls @ 1:40

6 x 50 Fist Drill @ 1:00
6 x 25 Build @ :30

8 x 100 Build
#1-4 w/fins @ 1:15/1:25
#5-8 IM @ 1:30/1:40

6 x 200 @ 2:55/3:10
Descend 1-3 Blue

6 x 100 @ 1:20/1:30
Descend 1-3
Ascend 4-6

4 x 100 Kick Red @ 1:30

Fri Dec 17 2021

400 IM
8 x 50 Kick @ :10 rest
10 x 100 @ :15 rest
Odds: Breast
Evens: Free

4 x 200 Kick @ 4:00
50 Kick Pink/50 Kick Red/50 Kick Pink/50 Kick Red
100 Kick Pink/100 Kick Red
100 Kick Red/100 Kick Pink
50 Kick Red/50 Kick Pink/50 Kick Red/50 Kick Pink

SPRINT

1 x 200 Paddle Pull Descend each 50   @ 4:00
4 x 50 25 MAX underwater kick/ 25 easy @ 1:00
4 x 25 (12.5 MAX kick/12.5 easy) @ :30

8 x 50 MAX @ 5:00

1 x 600
odd 100's: back
even 100's: (50 breast kick on back/50 free)

DISTANCE

1 x 300 w/fins
2 x 200 @ 2:30
#1 Build each 25 to Max FLIP
#2 Build each 50 to Pink

2 x {
4 x 100 Neg Split @ 1:30
(White/Pink)
4 x 50 Descend
4 x 25 Build
4 x 150 (breast/free/choice)
}
MID-DISTANCE

2 x (10 x 100 @ 2:30) ALL OUT MAX

Sat Dec 18 2021

4 x 200
#1 Free #2 Back/Breast by 50's #3 100 BK/100 Choice #4 Free

1 x 300 Kick
2 x 200 (100 White/100 Red Kick @ 3:30
6 x 50 D1-3 to Pink, 4-6 to MAX (start at White) @ 1:00

8 x 50 @ 1:00
Each one work one flip turns pushing off on back
4 x 100 JMI @ 1:10/1:15
#1-2 Neg Split (White/Red)
#2-4 DPS

1 x 800 Descend the 200's 1-4
(:30 rest)
2 x 600 White-Pink @ 7:30/7:45
(:30 rest)
1 x 500 (100 Pink/200 Red/100 Blue/100 MAX)

8 x 75 Chutes @ 1:30
25 no breath/50 Build

Mon Dec 20 2021

6 x 150 odds: Free evens: (50 Back/50 BR/50 Choice)
12 x 75
#1-4 IMO (Kick/Swim) @ 1:00
#5-8 Worst Stroke (Kick no board/drill) @ 1:00
#9-12

10 x 25 Build each 25 to fast flip @ 1:10
8 x 25 (12.5 underwater kick sprint/12.5 breakout MAX, easy) @ :30

1 x 200 Choice
6 x 50 Paddle @ :50

    SPRINT

1 x 300 FR/Non-FR by 50
3 x 100 IM (2) Pink (1) Red @ 1:10
4 x 50 JMI @ :40/:45
(2:00)
1 x 200 FR/Non-FR by 100
2 x 100 JMI Red-Blue @ 1:45
4 x 50 JMI Dolphin kick @ :55/1:00
(1:00)
1 x 100 FR Blue
1 x 100 IM White @ 1:45
4 x 50 1 Breath @ 1:20

    DISTANCE

10 x (50 + 50 easy)
500 Hold 500 Goal pace −1
200 Hold 200 Goal Pace
5 x (100 + 100 easy)
500 − Hold 500 Goal Pace
200 − Hold 200 Goal Pace + 2
3 x (200 + 100 easy)
D1-3

    MID-DISTANCE

5 x {
  400 @ 4:30/4:45/4:50
  4 x 100 Goal 500 Pace @ 1:10/1:15/1:20
  1:00 rest
  }

Tue Dec 21 2021

3 x 200 Free
1 x 100 Kick Fly
3 x 100 Freestyle

10 x 100 @ 1:30
odds: (25 kick/25 drill/50 swim with no breath turns)
evens: DPS

12 x 50 @ 40 JMI

5 x 100 @ 1:15/1:25
Keep all the same speed

1 x 200 Pink

Wed Dec 22 2021

1 x 300 Free
2 x 200 (100 Kick/100 Swim Non-Free)

8 x 50 @ 1:00
Each one work one flip turns pushing off on back
4 x 100 JMI @ 1:10/1:15
#1-2 Neg Split (White/Red)
#2-4 DPS

    SPRINT

4 x 200 Paddle w/Pull Buoy @ 2:40
#1 Descend each 100
#2 Build each 200
#3 Fast Flips
#4 DPS

8 x (100 + 50 easy)
D1-4 , D5-8

1 x 400 FR/Non-FR by 100
8 x 50 (2 white/ 2 pink/ 2 red/ 2 pink) @ :50
4 x 50 Worst Stroke @ 1:00
1 x 300 (50 BK/50 BR)
3 x 100 (2) Pink (1) Red @ 1:20
3 x 50 (25 underwater/25 easy) @ 1:00

1 x 200 (FR/Non-FR by 100)
2 x 100 (1) Red (1) Blue @ 1:20
2 x 50 #1 Stroke Drill @ 1:00

8 x 50 Kick MAX @ 1:00

    DISTANCE

8 x 100 Paddle w/Pull Buoy @ 1:15
4 x 25 (drill,build,drill,sprint) @ :40
1 x Broken 100 @ 25's or 200 @ 50's
2 x 50
10 x 75 @ 1:15
1-4 (swim/kick/non-free)
5-8 (easy,medium,build to fast finish) # 9-10 Pink

4 x 100 (50 Kick/50 swim) @ 1:40

    MID-DISTANCE

4 x 25 (Drill/Build/Drill/Drill/Sprint) @ :40
3 x Broken 500's
(:10 sec @ each 100)

Cooldown

Thu Dec 23 2021

2 x 300
#1 Free #2 RIMO (drill fly)
6 x 50 non-free @ :15 rest
5 x 100 Paddle w/Pull Buoy @ 1:30
6 x 50 Pull @ 1:00

4 x 75
Each 25 - 12.5 underwater kick/12.5 swim
4 x 25 underwater Kick @ :40

2 x 500 Paddle/Fins @ 6:00/6:30
#1 Build each 100 to MAX flip + 5 Strokes MAX no breath
#2 Descend 100's

8 x 100 JMI @ 1:15/1:20
4 x 25 Blue no breath @ :30
4 x 200 @ 2:20/2:30
odds: Ascend starting at Red
evens: Descend to Max no breath finish
(2:00)
3 x 100 @ 1:00/1:05

1 x 300 JMI @ 4:00/4:20
2 x 200 Kick @ 4:00/4:20
#1 Flutter #2 Dolphin
4 x 50 Red Swim @ 1:10/1:15

Fri Dec 24 2021

400 IM
8 x 50 Kick @ :10 rest
10 x 100 @ :15 rest
Odds: Fly
Evens: Free

3 x 600 @ + :15 rest
#1 Paddle/Pull
#2 Paddle
#3 Descend each 100 to Pink

    SPRINT

12 x 25 @ :55
5 x 50 MAX @ 4:00
#1-4 max of 1 breath
#10 No Breath

300 easy

    DISTANCE

1 x 800
(200 Pull/ 200 Swim/ 200 Pull/ 200 IM)
(1:00)
4 x 200 @ 2:20/2:40
Pink-Red-Blue-MAX

10 x 100
odds: Hold 500 goal pace @ 1:30
evens: White @ 1:35/1:40
2 x {
   8 x 50 @ :55
   (:30)
   4 x 25 underwater @ :45
}
    MID-DISTANCE

1 x (600 Pink + 200 easy)
4 x (300 + 100)
Descend
(1:00)
8 x (100 Red+ 100 easy)
(1:00)
4 x 200 All Red
(1:00)
8 x (50 + 50 easy)
Hold 1000 Goal Pace

Sat Dec 25 2021

1 x 400 IM
4 x 200 IM @ 2:50
9 x 100 @ 1:15 BP: 3-5

1000 Kick w/Board
2 x 200 IMO

4 x 200 Kick White @ 3:30

Paddle/Pull
1 x 400 easy @ :10
1 x 300 Moderate @ :10
1 x 200 fast @ :10
4 x 100 Free/Back @ 1:20/1:25
4 x 200 Free/Back @ 3:00 /3:30

Cooldown – 5 x 100 @ 1:40

Mon Dec 27 2021

200 SKIMPS
6 x 50 IMO @ 1:00

6 x 200
#1-2 (100 Back/100 Breast) @ +:20 rest
#3-4 Choice Swim @ 2:40
#5-6 (50 BK/100 Kick no board/50 Choice)

    SPRINT

3 x 200 Free @ 2:30 D1-3
4 x (100 Fast + 50 easy)
4 x (50 MAX + 50 easy)
    DISTANCE

1 x 600 Free
1 x 400 IM
8 x 50 IMO x 2 @ :10 rest

6 x 150 (Drill/Kick/Swim) @ 2:15
5 x 50 fist #1 Stroke @ 1:00
4 x 25 build to pink @ :30

1 x 400 IM @ 5:10/5:30/6:00/6:30
4 x 50 Kick no board IMO @ :45/:50
4 x 200 IM @ 3:00/3:15/3:30/3:40
8 x 50 kick no board #1 Stroke @ :50

8 x 50 Chutes @ 1:15/1:20
10 x 50 w/ fins (12.5 underwater kick/12.5 swim) @ 1:00

    MID-DISTANCE

2 x 400 White – Pink @ 4:00
4 x 100 D 1-4 @ 1:30
600 White
3 x 100 Work the Turns @ 1:30
2 x 300 Pink – Red @ 3:50
300 Negative Split

4 x 50 Build to great finish @ 1:00

Tue Dec 28 2021

1 x 500 (200 Free/200 Non-Free/100 RIMO)
8 x 100 @ :10 rest
odds: # 1 Stroke (50 drill/50 swim)
evens: (50 Bk/50 BR)

10 x 50 Kick @ :55
1 x 400 IM w/Fins
4 x 25 sprint kick @ :50

2 x 500 @ 5:40/6:00
#1 (250 White/ 250 Pink)
#2 (250 Red/ 250 Clear)
(1:00)
4 x 100 @ 1:30
White-Pink-Red-Blue
2 x 500 @ 5:40/6:00
#1 (250 White/250 Red)
#2 (250 Blue/250 White)
4 x 100 @ 1:30
Pink-Red-Blue-MAX

Wed Dec 29 2021

1 x 500 Free RB5
3 x 100 Kick
3 x 100 Free RB5

9 x 100
#1-3 D1-3 to Pink
#4-6 Bp 5/7 by 50
#7-9 Build each turn to MAX flip + 3 MAX Strokes Breakout

    SPRINT

2 x {
   2 x 200 @ 3:00
}
6 x 100 Descend , Hold time on 5-6 @ 1:20/1:30
6 x 50 Kick @ :50/:55

4 x 50 @ 3:30 MAX
2 x 400 @ 5:00/5:10

    DISTANCE

10 x 50 @ 4:00
#1-3 MAX of 3 Breaths
#4-6 MAX of 2 Breaths
#7-9 MAX of 1 Breath
#10 No Breath

4 x (75+ 25 easy)
Descend
8 x (50 + 50 easy)
Round 1 all red
Round 2 all MAX

    MID-DISTANCE

2 x 200 (White/Pink) @ 2:30
4 x 100 Choice @ 1:30
8 x 50 D 1-4, 5-8 @ 1:00
25's from a dive MAX
6 x 25 build to max finish
6 x 100 (Free/Non-Free) @ 1:40

Thu Dec 30 2021

1 x 100 SKIMPS

4 x 50 kick no board #1 stroke @ :50

6 x 75 w/fins (25 underwater kick/25 swim/25 underwater kick) @ 1:20
(1:00)

3 x 200 Free @ 2:30 D 1-3
4 x (100 Fast + 50 easy)

4 x 150 (Fly/Back/Breast) @ 2:00/2:10
Work Transition Turn + ½ way underwater on Transition
4 x 50 Red @ :40

8 x 50 w/chutes @ 1:20
#1-4 IMO D1-4 , #4-8 IMO Kick D1-4 to MAX

Fri Dec 31 2021

200 SKIMPS
8 x 50 @ 1:00
odds: RB:1
evens: RB:3

4 x 200 @ 2:30/2:40
odds: BP: 3,5 by 100
evens: BP: 3,7 by 50
(2:00)
3 x 300 w/fins @ 3:15/3:30
odds: DPS – lowest Stroke count
evens: kick ½ underwater on each wall
(2:00)

    SPRINT

5 x {
   200 Best Average @ 3:00
   4 x 50 Best Avg. @ :50 + 1:00 rest
}

    DISTANCE

5 x {
   400 @ 4:45/4:50
   4 x 100 Goal 500 Pace –1 @ 1:10/1:15/1:20
   1:00 rest
}

    MID-DISTANCE

1 x 1200 (300 White/300 Pink/(:30)/300 Red/300 Pink)
(:30)
4 x 100 JMI @ 1:05/1:10
1 x 800 (200 White/200 Pink/(:30)/200 Red/200 Pink)
(:30)
4 x 100 JMI @ 1:05/1:15
1 x 600 (200 White/200 Pink/200 Red)
(2:00)
5 x 100 Best Average @ 1:20/1:30

January 2022

1 Saturday
2 Sunday
3 Monday
4 Tuesday
5 Wednesday
6 Thursday
7 Friday
8 Saturday
9 Sunday
10 Monday
11 Tuesday
12 Wednesday
13 Thursday
14 Friday
15 Saturday
16 Sunday
17 Monday
18 Tuesday
19 Wednesday
20 Thursday
21 Friday
22 Saturday
23 Sunday
24 Monday
25 Tuesday
26 Wednesday
27 Thursday
28 Friday
29 Saturday
30 Sunday
31 Monday

Sat Jan 01 2022

1 x 300 Free
2 x 100 BackStroke
1 x 200 Free
2 x 100 Back

5 x 100 (Kick/Drill/Swim/Drill) @ 2:00
1 x 400 IMO w/Fins
4 x 25 underwater kick @ :30

3 x 400 IM @ :20
#1 50 Kick RED/50 Swim White
#2 Descend each 100 + 1/2 way under water MAX kick
#3 Descend 100's #1-3 to Pink, 4th 100 long streamline fast legs
2 x {
   12 x 50
   #1-6 Best Stroke @ :45/:55
   #7-12 Worst Stroke @ :50/:55
}
6 x 75 w/chutes (2)Fly-(2)Back-(2)Breast @ 1:20 Work under waters
4 x 100 Free w/fins JMI @ :55/1:00

Mon Jan 03 2022

4 x 200
Free-NonFree-Back/BR by 50's-Kick

4 x 75
Each 25 - 12.5 underwater kick/12.5 swim
4 x 25 underwater Kick @ :40

2 x 500 Paddle/Fins @ 6:00/6:30
#1 Build each 100 to MAX flip + 5 Strokes MAX no breath
#2 Descend 100's

   SPRINT

6 x 75 Build @ 1:15

1 x 400 pull @ 5:00
5 x 100 (3) White (2) Pink @ 1:30
1 x 300 (150 Kick no board/ 150 Swim) @ 5:30
5 x 50 (3) White (1) Pink (1) Red @ 1:00

   DISTANCE

3 x { @ 12:00
    1 x 200 @ 3:00 Dive
    Go 500 Pace
    2 x 100 @ 1:40
    Goal going out 200 pace for 500
    1 x 100 Dive MAX
}
10 x 50 @ 1:00
Odds 50 Kick
Evens 50 Swim

   MID-DISTANCE

3 x 300 @ 3:45/3:55
White-Pink-Red
4 x 100 JMI @ 1:10/1:20
(1:00)
4 x 100 @ 1:20/1:30
Red-Blue-(2) MAX
(2:00)
6 x 50 @ 1:00
DPS max of 5 Breaths @ 1:10

Tue Jan 04 2022

4 x 200 @ :15 rest
odds: Free
evens: (50 back drill/50 Choice)

3 x 100 Non-Free work walls @ 1:40

6 x 50 Fist Drill @ 1:00
6 x 25 Build @ :30

   2 x 300 Free JMI @ 3:15/3:30
4 x 50 Kick MAX @ 1:00
(1:00)
2 x 300 Free JMI @ 2:05/2:15
4 x 50 Kick MAX @ 1:00

Wed Jan 05 2022

1 x 100 SKIMPS

4 x 50 kick no board #1 stroke @ :50

4 x 75 (25 fist drill/25 swim/25 build) @ 1:20
8 x 50 (25 kick no board/25 swim) @ 1:00

   SPRINT

8 x 100 IM@ 1:20
3 x 300 @ 3:30/3:45
Descend
4 x 50 Easy @ 1:00
3 x 200 @ 2:20/2:30
Descend
4 x 50 Easy @ 1:00

   DISTANCE

2 x 500 @ 6:30/7:00/7:20
#1 Build each 50 to Pink
#2 3Descend each 100 starting at Pink

6 x 200
#1-2 IM @ 2:30/2:40/2:50
#3-4 Swim @ 2:20/2:30
#5-6 RIMO (drill fly) @ 2:30/2:40/2:50

2 x {
   1 x 300 @ 3:30/3:40/3:50
   4 x 50 @ :40
}
   MID-DISTANCE

5 x 200 Paddle/Pull Pink@ 3:00

4 x 100 IMO@ 1:40

1 x 500 White @ 6:15/6:30

4 x 200 D 1-4 @ 2:20
1 x 400 Pink @ 5:00/5:10
4 x 100 D 1-4 @ 1:30

Thu Jan 06 2022

200 SKIMPS

2 x {
   1 x 400 Kick
   4 x 50 Kick w/fins
}
4 x 100 @ 1:15/1:20
4 x 25 DPS @ :25
(:30)
4 x 100 Descend

8 x 50 w/fins (12.5 underwater Kick Red/12.5 Swim no breath/25 easy) @ 1:00
(1:00)
8 x 25 @ :40
odds: Build
evens: Accelerate

5 x 100 Negative Split (50 White/50 Blue) @ 1:20
Stroke - Free White/Stroke Blue
(1:00)
5 x 100 MAX Kick @ 2:00
(3:00)
5 x 100 D1-5 to MAX @ 1:20
All Stroke
(1:00)
5 x 50 MAX Kick @ 1:20
(3:00)

Fri Jan 07 2022

200 SKIMPS
6 x 50 IMO @ 1:00

9 x 100
#1-3 D1-3 to Pink
#4-6 Bp 5/7 by 50
#7-9 Build each turn to MAX flip + 3 MAX Strokes Breakout

SPRINT

12 x 25 @ :45
10 x 50 MAX @ 4:00
#1-3 max of 3 breaths
#4-6 max of 2 breaths
#7-9 max of 1 breath
#10 No Breath

300 easy

DISTANCE

4 x 200 (White/Pink/Red/Blue) @ 2:20/2:30/2:40/2:50/3:00
8 x 100 @ 1:20/1:25/1:40
D1-4 , 5-8 Hold Time
(2:00)
3 x 200 (Red/Blue/MAX) @ 2:30/2:40/2:50
6 x 100 Best Average @ 1:25/1:40

MID-DISTANCE

Mile MAX for time
2 x 400 Paddle w/Pull Buoy

Sat Jan 08 2022

1 x 400 Free
1 x 300 Non-Free
1 x 200 Kick
1 x 100 IM

6 x 50 Fist Drill @ 1:006 x 25 Build to great finish @ :30

2 x {
    1 x 300 Kick (150 White w/board/150 Pink no board) @ 5:45
    4 x 50 Descend to MAX @ 1:00
    4 x 25 Dolphin on back @ :30
}

5 x 100 @ 1:30

1 x 400 DPS @ 5:20
4 x 100 Choice 2 red/ 2 pink @ 1:50
(:30)
1 x 400 pull @ 5:00
2 x 100 (2) White (1) Pink
(:30)
1 x 400 pull @ 5:00
5 x 100 blue @ 1:20

Mon Jan 10 2022

1 x 300 Free
2 x 200 #1 Kick no board, #2 Kick Board
5 x 100 odds: IM, evens: Choice

6 x 200
#1-2 (100 Back/100 Breast) @ +:20 rest
#3-4 Choice Swim @ 2:40
#5-6 (50 BK/100 Kick no board/50 Choice)

   SPRINT

4 x 200 @ 3:00
(2) White (1) Pink
(1:00)
4 x 100 Pink – Red – Blue- MAX @ 1:20
2 x {
   8 x 50 @ :50
   (:30)
   4 x 25 underwater @ :40
}

   DISTANCE

8 x 50 (25 Drill/ 25 build to max finish) @ :50

1 x 400 BP: 3,5 by 100's @ 4:10
4 x 50 Non-Free @ :50
1 x 300 BP: 3,5,7 @ 3:50
4 x 50 kick no board @ 1:00
1 x 200 Kick Pink @ 4:00
4 x 50 D 1-4 to Pink @ 1:00

8 x 25 Breakout

   MID-DISTANCE

8 x 50 w/fins (12.5 underwater Kick Red/12.5 Swim no breath/25 easy) @ 1:00
(1:00)
8 x 25 @ :40
odds: Build
evens: Accelerate
8 x 100 Negative Split (50 White/50 Blue) @ 1:20FR/1:30 FR
(1:00)
5 x 100 MAX Kick @ 2:00
(3:00)
8 x 100 @ 1:25/1:30
(2) Pink-(2) Red-(2) Blue- (2) MAX
(1:00)
5 x 100 Pull Blue @ 1:30
(3:00)

Tue Jan 11 2022

400 IM
8 x 50 Kick @ :10 rest
10 x 100 @ :15 rest
Odds: Fly
Evens: Free

2 x {
   4 x 25 fist drill
   2 x 25 Stroke build
}
4x 25 (drill/build/drill/sprint) @ :40

6 x 100 JMI @ 1:20/1:30
odds: #1 Stroke
evens: IM
2 x (4 x 25 IMO Blue no breath on Fly/Free) @ :30
(2:00)

4 x {
   100 IM w/chute @ 1:40/1:50
   75 Fly Descend @ 1:10/1:15
   50 Back (25 kick underwater/25 swim) @ :50/:55
   25 Breast DPS w/ MAX kick @ :30
   50 Free MAX @ 3:00
}

Wed Jan 12 2022

400 IM
8 x 50 Kick @ :10 rest
10 x 100 @ :15 rest
Odds: Back
Evens: Free

3 x 300 @ 3:45/3:55
(1:00)
8 x 25 Paddles DPS – Count Stroke per 25 @ :45
4 x 25 Keep Same Stroke Count as w/ paddles per 25

5 x 50 drill @ 1:00

4 x 25 Kick Build each 25 @ :40
4 x 50 Kick Descend @ :55
4 x 25 Kick @ :30

9 x 50 (2 @ :40, 1 @ :30)

    SPRINT

1 x 300 Work each breakout

3 x {
1 x 100 MAX @ 7:00
2 x 50 MAX @ 4:00
}
1 x 500 Free @ :20
5 x 50 Non-Free @ :50
1 x 400 Build each 100 to MAX finish @ :20
4 x 50 Non-Free @ :50

    DISTANCE

5 x (200 Best Average @ 3:10 + 4 x 50 Best Avg. @ :50 + 1:00 rest)

    MID-DISTANCE

2 x Broken 500's
3 x Broken 200's

Thu Jan 13 2022

6 x 150 odds: Free evens: (50 Back/50 BR/50 Choice)
12 x 75
#1-4 IMO (Kick/Swim) @ 1:00
#5-8 Worst Stroke (Kick no board/drill) @ 1:00
#9-12

2 x 300
#1 Scull
#2 (BK/Breast/Scull) by 100's

8 x 75 (Kick-Drill-Swim) @ 1:10
Sprint
3 x 200 w/fins DPS @ 2:30

8 x 100 w/fins @ 1:30
8 x 75 IMO @ 1:30 ex:
#1-2 50 FL Build + 25 BK MAX 15m
4 x { IMO
    2 x 100 @ 1:10/1:20
    1 x 200 Drill @ :30 rest
    4 x (50 + 50 easy)
    Add up to Best time 200
}

Fri Jan 14 2022

300 FR
200 Kick
100 IM
1 x 500 Paddle/Pull

3 x 100 Non-Free work walls @ 1:40

6 x 50 Fist Drill @ 1:00
6 x 25 Build @ :30

    SPRINT

3 x 200 Paddle/Pull @ 2:45
3 x 100 Pull @ 1:20

6 x 25 w/ fins (12.5 underwater MAX kick) @ :30

4 x 50 Max @ 3:00
4 x 25 blue

1 x 400 easy
2 x (5 x 50 Best Average) @ 1:30
second round w/ fins

    DISTANCE

4 x 100 IM pink @ 1:50

1 x 200 Broken each 50 for :10
(1:00)
3 x 50 MAX from a dive @ 2:30 rest
4 x 25 MAX breakout @ :10 rest

1 x 400 White @ 4:00/4:10
4 x 100 Kick D 1-4 @ 1:50
5 x 100 (25 kick BR/25 swim choice) @ 1:40

    MID-DISTANCE

8 x 50 build to great finish @ 1:00

10 x 100 @ 1:30 Best Average
2 x Broken 500
1 x 100 Red @ 1:40
1 x 200 Pink @ 2:40
1 x 100 Blue @ 1:40
1 x 100 MAX @ 1:40

Sat Jan 15 2022

3 x 400
#1 (200 Free/200 Back) @ :20 rest
#2 (200 Kick/200 Free) @ :20 rest
#3 (200 Choice/200 Kick no board)

12 x 75 @
#1-4 (50 Free/25 BK)
#5-8 (25 Kick no board/50 Breast)
#9-12 (Fly/Back/Breast)

4 x 200 Paddle/Pull

8 x 50 @ :50

IM
200 IM (50 Kick/50 Swim) @ 4:00

6 x 25 w/chutes @ 1:10
D1-6
(1:00)
6 x 25 w/chutes Build@ :45
4 x 25 w/chutes MAX@ :45

6 x 25 w/fins underwater kick @ :30
4 x 50 IMO @ :45/:50
4 x 100 Free Bp 5@ 1:30/1:40
(2:00)
3 x 100 IM @ 1:20/1:30
4 x 50 IMO @ :45/:50

(1:00)
6 x 50 w/fins Fast kick dolphin @ 1:00
1 x 400 w/fins dolphin on back

Mon Jan 17 2022

4 x 200
Free-NonFree-Back/BR by 50's-Kick

6 x 100
#1-3 (Kick/Drill/Swim) @ 2:00
#4-6 Past flags on each wall @ 2:00

SPRINT

4 x 200 @ 3:00
(2) White (1) Pink
(1:00)
4 x 100 Pink – Red – Blue- MAX @ 1:20
2 x { 8 x 50 (2 @ :35, 1 @ :50)
    (:30)
     4 x 25 underwater @ :40
}

DISTANCE

1 x (600 + 200 easy) Pink
4 x (300 + 100)
D 1-4 to Pink
4 x (200 + 50 easy)
White-Pink-Red-Red
8 x (100 + 50 easy)
All Red
8 x (50 + 50 easy)
Hold Goal 500 Pace

MID-DISTANCE

1 x 600 Paddle w/Pull Buoy
10 x 100 JMI @ 1:10/1:25
3 x {
   1 x 75 Build @ 1:20
   2 x 50 @ :50
   1 x 500 Paddle w/Pull Buoy
   2 x 200 @ 2:30/2:40
   Pink-Red
}
2 x {
   600 Choice
   6 x 50 @ 1:00
   White Pink Red Blue (2)Max
}

Tue Jan 18 2022

500 SKIMPS
4 x 100 IM @ 1:20/1:40

3 x 400
#1 Paddle w/Pull Buoy @ 5:00/5:10/5:20
#2 Swim BP: 3,5 by 100 @ 4:40/4:50/5:00
#3 Swim (75 Free/25 Back w/1/2 underwater kick)

5 x 200 Best Average @ 3:30/4:00
3 x 100 @ 1:30 easy
3 x 400 @ 5:20
Clear-White-Pink
4 x 50 Kick MAX @ 1:00
(1:00)
4 x 300 @ 3:30/3:40
(1)Pink - (2) Red – (1)Blue
4 x 50 Kick MAX

Wed Jan 19 2022

200 SKIMPS
8 x 50 @ 1:00
odds: RB:1
evens: RB:3

2 x {
   8 x 50 Kick #1 Stroke D1-4 , 5-8 to MAX
   1 x 400 Kick no board
}

     SPRINT

8 x 100 White @ 1:20
4 x 50 @ :40
6 x 100 IM @ 1:30
4 x 50 @ :40

2 x {
   1 x 200 @ 2:30
   4 x 50 @ 1:00
   Descend Descend
}
1 x 50 w/fins from push, MAX

    DISTANCE

5 x 200 MAX

    MID-DISTANCE

4 x 200
#1-2 IM Descend, #2-4 Ascend Free

6 x 200 @ 2:30/2:50
#1-2 200 Pink – 25 Blue
#3-4 200 Red – 25 MAX
#5-6 200 Red – 25 Red max of 2 breaths

10 x (100 + 50 easy)
Goal 1000 Pace
10 x (50 + 50 easy)
Goal 500 Pace –2

Thu Jan 20 2022

4 x 200
IM-NonFree-Free-Kick

3 x {
   1 x 300 – Catchup Drill
   5 x 50 drill – Choice @ 1:10
   4 x 25 Stroke @:40
}
10 x 50 w/fins 25 underwater kick/25 swim @ 1:00
4 x 25 underwater kick @ :40

3 x {   100 Red from Blocks
   200 easy
   100 MAX from push
   100 easy
    }

1 x 400 (100 Free/100 Back)
2 x 200 (Choice drill)

2 x {
   1 x 25 MAX from Dive @ :30
   1 x 75 JMI @ 1:10/1:15
   1 x 50 kick ½ way underwater on every wall @ :40/:45
   1 x 25 MAX underwater kick from Dive @ :40
   1 x 100 MAX for time
}
Cooldown
3 x 200 choice @ 3:00

Fri Jan 21 2022

1 x 600 (300 Free-300 NonFree)
4 x 100 IMO (drill fly) @ :10 rest
8 x 50 (Fly/Free, Back/Free, Breast/Free, Free/Free) @

6 x 50 Fist Drill @ 1:006 x 25 Build to great finish @ :30

2 x {
   1 x 300 Kick (150 White w/board/150 Pink no board) @ 5:45
   4 x 50 Descend to MAX @ 1:00
   4 x 25 Dolphin on back @ :30
}

    SPRINT

1 x 500 (200 Free White/200 Free Pink/100 Free Build Finish)
4 x 50 Kick Build to Pink @ 1:00
1 x 300 (150 Free White/150 Non-Free) @
4 x 50 fist drill @ 1:10
8 x 25 build Stroke @ :40

    DISTANCE

10 x (50+50 easy)
500 – Hold 500 Goal pace –2
200 – Hold 200 Goal pace – 1
5 x (100 + 100 easy)
500 – Hold 500 Goal Pace
200 – Hold 200 goal pace +1
3 x (200 + 100 easy)
D 1-3

    MID-DISTANCE

3 x 500 @ :15 rest
#1 Paddle/Pull
#2 Pull BP:5
#3 Pink
8 x (200 + 50 easy)
#1-2 White
#3-4 Pink
#5-7 Red
#8 MAX
4 x 100 easy @ 1:45

Sat Jan 22 2022

1 x 500 White Kick
Non-Stop{
    400 Kick-400 Pull-400 Swim
    300 Kick-300 Pull-300 Swim
    200 Kick- 200 Pull- 200 Swim
    100 Kick- 100 Pull- 100 Swim
}

10 x 25 w/ chutes @ :45 Red
10 x 25 x/ fins MAX underwater kick @ :30
2 x {
    4 x 200 @ 2:30
    (1:00)
}

5 x 100 @ 1:25/1:35
Keep all the same speed

Mon Jan 24 2022

200 SKIMPS
12 x 50 Drill IMO x 3 @ 1:00

4 x 100 IMO (Kick/Drill/Swim/Drill) @ 2:20
3 x 200 Free
4 x 25 kick red @ :30

      SPRINT

4 x 125 @ 1:50
6 x 25 accelerate @ :30

15 x 100 @ 1:30/1:40
#1-5 Negative Split (White/Blue)
#6-10 Descend to MAX
#7-15 Hold Best Average

1 x 300
2 x 200 @ 2:40
White Swim-White Kick
4 x 50 (Drill/Swim) @ 1:00

1x50 MAX from dive

      DISTANCE

8 x 50 (25 Drill/ 25 build to max finish) @ :50

1 x 100 Broken @ 25's
2 x 50 MAX
4 x 25 MAX

8 x 200 (free/kick/non-free/drill) @ 2:40
6 x 100 (Back/free/choice) @ + :10

      MID-DISTANCE

100 Pink
200 (Goal Time -Pink 100 x 2 + 3) @ 2:20/2:30
300 (Goal Time -200 + Pink 100 + 4) @ 4:00/4:30
400 (Goal Time -300 + Pink 100 + 5) @ 5:20/6:00

100 Red
200 (Goal Time -Red 100 x 2 + 2) @ 2:20/2:30
300 (Goal Time -200 + Red 100 + 3) @ 4:00/4:30
400 (Goal Time -300 + Red 100 + 4) @ 5:20/6:00

Tue Jan 25 2022

1 x 600 (300 Free-300 NonFree)
4 x 100 IMO (drill fly) @ :10 rest
8 x 50 (Fly/Free, Back/Free, Breast/Free, Free/Free) @

2 x {
   4 x 50 fist drill @ 1:00
   4 x 25 build @ :30
}
8 x 50 Kick @ 1:00
D1-4 , 5-8 to MAX (start at Pink)

RACE PACE
50 Free
100 Fly
100 Free
200 IM
200 Free
100 Back
500 Free
100 Breast

Wed Jan 26 2022

1 x 300 Free
2 x 100 BackStroke
1 x 200 Free
2 x 100 Back

5 x 100 @ 1:30
#1-2 Max of 2 breaths each 25
#3-4 (50 Free/50 Back)
#5 Max of 2 breaths each 25

SPRINT

2 x 300 DPS @ 4:00
5 x 100 (3) White (2) Pink @ 1:30
1 x 300 (150 Kick no board/ 150 Swim) @ 5:30
5 x 100 (3) White (1) Pink (1) Red @ 1:30

DISTANCE

4 x 200 Max for time, from dive

MID-DISTANCE

4 x 500 @ 6:00/6:10
1 white, 1 pink, 2 red
5 x 300 RED @ 3:50
12 x 50 D 1-6 , 7-12 to MAX @ :50

Thu Jan 27 2022

1 x 500 Free RB5
3 x 100 Kick
3 x 100 Free RB5

1 x 300 Scull
4 x 50 Dolphin on Back @ :50

4 x 100 (Kick/Drill) Worst Stroke @ 1:50
1 x 700 Paddle/Pull

4 x 100 IM @ 1:25
4 x 50 Fast Kick @ 1:00
1 x 200 easy
10 x 100 MAX Kick @ 1:40
500 Cooldown

Fri Jan 28 2022

3 x200
#1 Free
#2 (Back/Breast by 50's)
#3 (100 Choice/100 IM)

10 x 25 Build each 25 to fast flip @ 1:10
8 x 25 (12.5 underwater kick sprint/12.5 breakout MAX, easy) @ :30

SPRINT

2 x (300 + 100 easy)
White-Pink
4 x (50 + 50 easy)
All Kick Descend
(2:00)
2 x 300 IM @ 4:20
4 x (100 + 100 easy)
All Kick Descend to MAX
(2:00)
8 x 100 @ 1:40
50 Kick/50 Swim
8 x 50 (25 BK/25 Choice)

DISTANCE

2 x 400 (200 White Free/200 Pink BK) @ 5:30/5:40
4 x 100 IM @ 1:30/1:45
5 x 50 drill @ 1:00
(1:00)
3 x 200 Fin Swim @ 2:15/2:20
6 x 50 w/fins under/over @ 1:00

6 x 100
odds: JMI Free @ 1:10/1:15
evens: IM @ 1:15/1:20

MID-DISTANCE

1 x 800
(200 Pull/ 200 Swim/ 200 Pull/ 200 IM)
(1:00)
4 x 200 @ 2:20/2:30
Pink-Red-Blue-MAX

10 x 100
odds: Hold 500 goal pace @ 1:30
evens: White @ 1:35/1:40

2 x {
   8 x 50 @ :45
     (:30)
   4 x 25 underwater @ :40
}

Sat Jan 29 2022

600 Free
6 x 100 IM D1-3 and 4-6 @ 1:30

10 x 100 (25 drill/50 swim/25 drill) @ 1:30

8 x 50 @ :50
odds: build into first wall, great turn
evens: build into finish, great finish

2 x {
   4 x 25 (drill,build,drill,MAX) @ :40
}

4 x 50 #1 drill, #2 build, #3 drill, #4 sprint @ :45
3 x 100 (white/pink/red) @ 1:40
2 x 100 Pink – Red @ 1:30
4 x 50 D 1-4 @ 1:15
6 x 25 build to max finish

Mon Jan 31 2022

1 x 500 (200 Free/200 Non-Free/100 RIMO)
8 x 100 @ :10 rest
odds: # 1 Stroke (50 drill/50 swim)
evens: (50 Bk/50 BR)

1 x 300 (150 Kick no board/ 150 Swim) @ 5:30
1 x 500 white
2 x 300 Pull @ 3:45/4:00
10 x 50 @ 1:00
Odds 50 Free
Evens 50 Non Free

SPRINT

4 x 25 MAX

8 x 100 Best Average @ 1:20
1 x 300 Easy
2x(5 x 50 D1-5 to MAX) :10
5 x 200 Best Average @ 2:40

DISTANCE

3 x 200 w/fins DPS @ 2:20/2:30
3 x 400 Clear-White-Pink 5:00
3 x 300 White-Pink-Red   4:00
3 x 200 Pink-Red-Blue   3:00
3 x 100 Red-Blue-MAX   1:20

MID-DISTANCE

5 x 100 Neg Split (Clear-Pink) @ 1:20
Work long turns

5 x 200 BEST AVERAGE @ 2:20/2:30
10 x 100 BEST AVERAGE @ 1:30
4 x 50 MAX @ 1:00

1 x 200 easy

4 x 50 kick MAX @ 1:00

February 2022
1 Tuesday
2 Wednesday
3 Thursday
4 Friday
5 Saturday
6 Sunday
7 Monday
8 Tuesday
9 Wednesday
10 Thursday
11 Friday
12 Saturday
13 Sunday
14 Monday
15 Tuesday
16 Wednesday
17 Thursday
18 Friday
19 Saturday
20 Sunday
21 Monday
22 Tuesday
23 Wednesday
24 Thursday
25 Friday
26 Saturday
27 Sunday
28 Monday

Tue Feb 01 2022

1 x 400 (200 Free/200 Back)
1 x 300 (150 Kick non-free/150 kick breast)
1 x 200 (100 BK/100 Choice)
1 x 100 IM

8 x 75 @ 1:30
odds: Free drill
evens: Non-Free drill

2 x 8 x 50 (25 Drill/ 25 build to max finish) @ :50
6 x 100 Kick w/fins @ 1:20/1:30
25 underwater kick/25 dolphin on back/50 kick choice

2 x Broken 200's

2 x {
    1 x 75 MAX :30 rest
    1 x 25 MAX Kick :45-1:00 rest
    1 x 50 MAX Dive
}
3 x 400 @ :20 rest
#1 White/Pink #2 Kick #3 Build each 100
4 x 100 (50 Kick/50 Swim) @ 1:40

Wed Feb 02 2022

1 x 400 Kick
4 x 100 Kick (50 pink/50 red) @ 1:50
4 x 50 MAX Kick @ 1:00
1 x 200 easy

SPRINT

12 x 50 (2 easy @ 1:00, 1 FAST @ 1:00)

1 x 200 Pull @ 3:00
4 x 50 Kick @ 1:00
odds: White-Pink-Red
Evens: Red-Pink-White
(1:00)

1 x 400 Pull @ 5:00
4 x 100 Kick @ 1:40
Descend to MAX start @ Pink
(2:00)

2 x 200 Swim @ 2:30
(2:00)
2x 200 Kick w/fins @ 2:20/2:30

DISTANCE

4 x 300 w/ fins @ 3:40/3:50
(:30)
4 x 100 IM @ 1:30
4 x 50 @ 1:00
No breath into and out of each turn
4 x 25 MAX breakout @ :30
10 x 50 MAX @ 4:00

MID-DISTANCE

1 x 400 Free
4 x 100 IMO (optional drill fly) @ :10 rest
8 x 50 (Fly/Free, Back/Free, Breast/Free, Free/Free) @ :20
6 x 150 (drill/kick/swim) @ 2:10
6 x 50 fist drill #1 Stroke @ 1:00
4 x 25 Build

1 x 400 IM @ 5:40/6:10/6:30
4 x 50 Kick no board IMO @ :50
(2:00)
4 x 200 IM @ 3:15/3:30/3:40
8 x 50 Kick no board #1 Stroke @ :50

8 x 50 Kick Pink @ :55
4 x 50 IMO @ :50
4 x 100 Kick w/ chutes @ :30 sec rest

Thu Feb 03 2022

200 SKIMPS
8 x 50 @ 1:00
odds: RB:1
evens: RB:3

10 x 25 w/ chutes @ :45 Red
10 x 25 x/ fins MAX underwater kick @ :30
2 x {
   4 x 200 @ 2:30
   (1:00)
}

IM
3 x 300 IMO @ 4:10/4:204 x 50 BR Pull @ :55/1:00
3 x 150 (100 BR/50 BACK) @ 2:20/2:10
4 x 50 BK Pull @ :50/:55
4 x 75 (50 Back/25 Fly) @ 1:00/1:05
4 x 50 FL Pull @ :50/:55

Fri Feb 04 2022

200 SKIMPS
8 x 50 IMO @ :50
300 White

1 x 600 Paddle/Pull
Bp 5 by 100's work on great turns
1 x 400

　　　SPRINT

4 x 50s RED
2 x 50 MAX from Dive

1 x 400 Fin Swim

3 x 25 Chutes underwater kick w/fins

3 x 300 @ 4:00
3 x 100 D1-3 @ 1:20

　　　DISTANCE

4 x 200 @ 2:40, 2:50
Descend Each 200 + 25 Blue
(1:00)
8 x 75 @ :50/:55FR, 1:00/1:10BK & BR
(2:00)
4 x 200 @ 2:30/2:40 FR, 2:40/2:50BK, 2:50/3:00BR
#1-2 Negative Split
#3-4 Best time + 12
(2:00)
5 x 100 JMI @ 1:00/1:05/1:10

　　　MID-DISTANCE

5 x {
　　400 @ 4:30/4:45/4:50
　　4 x 100 Goal 500 Pace −1 @ 1:10/1:15/1:20
　　1:00 rest
}

Sat Feb 05 2022

1 x 500 (200 Free/200 Non-Free/100 RIMO)
8 x 100 @ :10 rest
odds: #1 Stroke (50 drill/50 swim)
evens: (50 Bk/50 BR)

4 x 100 IMO (Kick/Drill/Swim/Drill) @ 2:20
3 x 200 Free
4 x 25 kick red @ :30

4 x 50 Free @ :35/:40
4 x 100 Free @ 1:10/1:20
4 x 50 Free @ :35/:40
4 x 100 JMI @ 1:00/1:05/1:10/1:15
200 easy

Mon Feb 07 2022

4 x 200 Paddle w/Pull Buoy @ 2:20/2:30/2:40
8 x 100 (25 Build/50 Pink/25 Build to Fast Finish) @ 1:40
8 x 50 @ 1:00
#1-3 (1/2 underwater Kick + breakout on each wall)
#4-6 Build max of 3 breaths
#7-8 DPS

   SPRINT

3 x {
    300 DPS @ 4:00
    2 x 200 White-Pink @ 2:30
    3 x 100 Choice @ 1:30
    4 x 50 D 1-4 @ 1:00
    }

   DISTANCE

1 x 400 (100 Free/100 Back)
2 x 200 Stroke @ 2:45
Pink – Red
4 x 50 (12.5 underwater MAX kick + MAX breakout/12.5 easy swim) @ 1:00

2 x {
    1 x 25 MAX from Dive @ :35/:40
    1 x 75 JMI @ 1:10/1:15
    1 x 50 kick ½ way underwater on every wall @ :40/:45
    1 x 25 MAX underwater kick from Dive @ :40
    1 x 100 MAX for time
}
6 x 100 @ 1:40

   MID-DISTANCE

4 x 400 D 1-4 @ 4:40/5:00
1 x 800 Strong @ 9:30/10:00
8 x 100 @ 1:05/1:10

Tue Feb 08 2022

600 Free
3 x 100 Kick w/Board
10 x 100 IM Order @ :15 rest

10 x 25 w/ chutes @ :45 Red
10 x 25 x/ fins MAX underwater kick @ :30
2 x {
   4 x 200 @ 2:30
   (1:00)
}

2 x 300 @ 3:35/4:00
4 x 300 @ 3:45/4:25
2 x 100 @ 1:25/1:30
6 x 50 @ 1:00
500 easy

Wed Feb 09 2022

500 Free
6 x 100 IM @ :15 rest
4 x 100 Kick IM Order

8 x 50 @ 1:00
Each one work one flip turns pushing off on back
4 x 100 JMI @ 1:10/1:15
#1-2 Neg Split (White/Red)
#2-4 DPS

   SPRINT

2 x 200 (100 White/100 Red) @ 3:00/3:10
2 x 200 (100 Pink/100 Red) @ 3:00/3:10

2 x {
    2 x 100 JMI @ 1:40
    4 x 50 Red @ 1:05/1:10/1:15
    8 x 25 Max @ 1:00
    odds: from Dive
    evens: from Push
}
4 x 100 Descend to MAX @ 1:20/1:40

   DISTANCE

4 x 75 Kick @ 1:30
odds: White-Pink-Red
evens: Red-Pink-White

8 x 25 Sprints @ :30

5 x 100 @ 7:00 MAX
1 x 100 w/fins MAX go best time

   MID-DISTANCE

2 x {
    1 x 500 Pink + 100 easy
    1 x 400 Red + 100 easy
    1 x 300 Blue + 100 easy
    1 x 200 Red + 100 easy
    1 x 100 MAX + 100 easy
}

Thu Feb 10 2022

1 x 300 Free
2 x 200 #1 Kick no board, #2 Kick Board
5 x 100 odds: IM, evens: Choice

1 x 300 Scull
4 x 50 Dolphin on Back @ :50

4 x 100 (Kick/Drill) Worst Stroke @ 1:50
1 x 700 Paddle/Pull

3 x 400 IM w/fins FL & FR - BP: 3,5 by 50 @ 6:30
3 x 100 Fly/Back/BR @ 1:20

2 x {
   3 x 200 Paddle w/Pull Buoy
   6 x 100 @ 1:05/1:10/1:15 (IM)
}

Fri Feb 11 2022

1 x 500 White Kick
Non-Stop{
    400 Kick-400 Pull-400 Swim
    300 Kick-300 Pull-300 Swim
    200 Kick- 200 Pull- 200 Swim
    100 Kick- 100 Pull- 100 Swim
}

4 x 75 (25 fist drill/25 swim/25 build) @ 1:20
8 x 50 (25 kick no board/25 swim) @ 1:00

    SPRINT

4 x 300 w/fins @ 3:45

2 x {
    4 x 100 @ 1:25
    #1-2 Descend each 100 to Pink
    #3-4 Descend each 100
}
4 x 50's MAX @ 3:00
4 x 25's MAX @ 2:00

4 x 125 Neg Split (75 White/75 Red) @ 2:00
4 x 100 Descend to MAX @ 1:30
4 x 100 Best Average @ 1:30

    DISTANCE

4 x {
    1 x 75 MAX
    (:30)
    50 MAX from push
}

1 x 300 Easy
2 x 200 @ 2:30
White-Pink
8 x 25 w/fins Underwater @ :40

    MID-DISTANCE

8 x 75 @ 1:15
Odds: Work Turns
 Evens: Work Finish
1 x 600 (3 x 100 White/100 Red)
3 x (400 + 100 easy)
D 1-3
3 x (200 + 50 easy)
D 1-3
5 x 100 Blue + 50 easy
3 x 200 Blue + 100 easy

Sat Feb 12 2022

1 x 400 (200 Free/200 Non-Free)
1 x 300 Kick
1 x 200 RIMO (drill fly)

1 x 300 Scull

2 x {
   4 x 50 Fist Drill @ 1:10
   2 x 25 Build to Pink @ :30
}

2 x {
   1 x 25 MAX from Dive @ :30
   1 x 100 JMI @ 1:15/1:25
   1 x 50 kick ½ way underwater on every wall @ :40/:45
   1 x 25 MAX underwater kick from Dive @ :40
   1 x 100 MAX for time
}

Mon Feb 14 2022

1 x 500 (200 Free/200 Non-Free/100 RIMO)
8 x 100 @ :10 rest
odds: # 1 Stroke (50 drill/50 swim)
evens: (50 Bk/50 BR)
6 x 200
#1-2 (100 Back/100 Breast) @ +:20 rest
#3-4 Choice Swim @ 2:40
#5-6 (50 BK/100 Kick no board/50 Choice)

    SPRINT

6 x 100 (white/pink/red/blue) @ 1:25

8 x 25 from a dive w/ 5 Strokes fast @ 1:00 rest

1 x 100 Broken @ the 50 and the 75 @ 4:00 rest
2 x 50 MAX from a dive @ 2:30 rest
4 x 25's Max start + breakout, easy remainder

1 x 500 White @ 6:30/7:00
4 x 100 Kick D 1-4 @ 1:50
5 x 50 (25 kick BR/25 swim choice) @ 1:00

    DISTANCE

4 x 50 Kick no board RED @ :50
(:30)
4 x 200 @ 2:10/2:20
White-Pink-(2) Red
4 x 50 Kick no board BLUE@ :50
(1:00)
8 x 100 JMI @ 1:05/1:10

    MID-DISTANCE

3 x (500 + 100 easy)
#1 Paddle/Pull - White
#2 Paddle - Pink
#3 Swim - Red

3 x (300 + 100 easy)
White-Pink-(2) Red
(1:00)
1 x (200 MAX + 100 easy)
3 x (200 + 100 easy)
Pink-Red-Blue
(1:00)
1 x (100 MAX + 100 easy)

2 x (100 + 50 easy)
Pink-Red
1 x (50 MAX + 50 easy)

Tue Feb 15 2022

400 RIMO
6 x 100 Non-Free (50 Kick/50 Swim) @ :10 rest

8 x 50 @ 1:00
Each one work one flip turns pushing off on back
4 x 100 JMI @ 1:10/1:15
#1-2 Neg Split (White/Red)
#2-4 DPS

4 x 75 Build each @ 1:20
4 x 25 MAX Breakout @ :40

6 x 50 w/fins Fast kick dolphin @ 1:10
6 x 25 w/fins underwater kick @ :30
(1:00)
6 x 25 w/chutes JMI @ :50
6 x 25 w/chutes Build @ :40
4 x 25 w/chutes MAX @ :40

4 x 100 w/fins dolphin on back @ 1:30

400 Free @ 4:50/5:10
4 x 50 red @ :50
300 BP 7 by 50's @ 3:40/3:50
(2:00)
4 x 100 Choice @ 1:30/1:40
4 x 50 Blue @ :40
1 x 200 BP: 7

Wed Feb 16 2022

1 x 200 Kick Breast
1 x 200 Kick Fly
1 x 200 Back
1 x 200 Kick Free

8 x 50 (25 Drill/25 Swim Stroke) @ 1:00

2 x 4 x 50 Catchup @ 1:10

   SPRINT

4 x kick w/fins underwater
2 x 200 White @ 3:00

100 @ 1:20/1:30
(2) @ 1:10 or faster
(2) @ 1:08 or faster
(2) @ 1:05 or faster
(1) @ 1:02 or faster
(1) @ 1:00 or faster
(1) @ :59 or faster
(1) @ :58 or faster
(1) @ :57 or faster
(1) @ :56 or faster
(1) @ :54 or faster
(1) @ :52
(1) @ :50

   DISTANCE

6 x 125 w/fins (25 kick/50 swim/25 kick/25 dolphin on back) @ 1:50

2 x 300 White @ 4:00
4 x 50 D 1-4 @ 1:00
2 x 200 Pink-Red @ 2:40
4 x 50 D 1-4 @ 1:00
2 x 100 White @ 1:35
4 x 50 Max Breakout @ 1:35

6 x 50 Kick D1-4 , Hold time on 5-6

   MID-DISTANCE

600 (300 White Free/300 Pink Back) @ 9:00
4 x 200 IM @ 2:40/2:45(1:00)
2 x 400 Fin Swim @ :20 rest
odds: BP: 5
evens: BP: 4
6 x 50 under/over w/fins @ 1:00
5 x 100 JMI @ 1:15
odds: (50 Free/50 Non-Free)
evens: Free

Thu Feb 17 2022

1 x 300 Free
2 x 200 (100 Kick/100 Swim Non-Free)

5 x 200 :20
#1 Kick
#2 Paddle w/Pull Buoy White
#3 Paddle w/Pull Buoy Pink
#4 Paddle w/Pull Buoy Red
#5 Kick

2 x 300 (200 Free/100 IM)
1 x 300 Kick no board
8 x 75 2 of each Stroke kick/drill/swim by 25's @ 1:15

5 x 200 Pull @ 2:30/2:45
odds: BP: 3
evens: BP: 5

1 x 200 kick no board @ 3:15
4 x 75 @ 1:20
   odds: easy/medium/fast
   evens:fast/medium/easy

2 x {
1 x 400 w/fins @ 5:00
4 x 50 kick dolphin on back @ :45
}
16 x 25 w/fins underwater kick @ :40
8 x 75 w/ chutes @ 1:20

Cooldown

Fri Feb 18 2022

8 x 100 @ 1:30
odds: Free
evens: (50 Fly drill/50 Choice)

10 x 75 continuous IM @ 1:10

     SPRINT

4 x 50 @ :50

1 x 100 MAX
1 x 50 MAX
1 x 25 MAX
1 x 50 MAX
1 x 100 MAX

2 x 200 Pink@ 2:20
1 x 400 Pink @ 7:20
4 x 50 White @ 1:10

     DISTANCE

1 x 200 (100 Red/100 Pink)
(:30)
4 x 100 JMI @ 1:00/1:10

1 x 300 (100 White/100 Pink/100 Red)
(:30)
4 x 75 JMI @ :50/:55

2 x 200 (100 Pink/100 Red) @ 2:30
(1:00)
3 x 100 Best Average @ 2:00

     MID-DISTANCE

1 x (600 + 200 easy) Pink
4 x (300 + 100)
D 1-4 to Pink
4 x (200 + 50 easy)
White-Pink-Red-Red
8 x (100 + 50 easy)
All Red
8 x (50 + 50 easy)
Hold Goal 1000 Pace

Sat Feb 19 2022

2 x 400
#1 Free #2 IM by 100's

3 x 200
#1 RIMO #2 IM #3 Choice

10 x 25 Build each 25 to fast flip @ 1:10
8 x 25 (12.5 underwater kick sprint/12.5 breakout MAX, easy) @ :30

1 x 200 Choice
6 x 50 Paddle @ :50

2 x 800 @ 10:00/11:00
White-Pink-Red-White by 100s
4 x 50 Kick Descend to MAX @ :55
(1:00)
2 x 500 @ 5:30/6:00
Pink - Red
4 x 50 Kick D1-4 at MAX @ 1:00
(2:00)
2 x 300 @ 3:30/3:45
Red-MAX
4 x 50 Kick Dolphin on back @ 1:00

Mon Feb 21 2022

3 x 400
#1 (200 Free/200 Back) @ :20 rest
#2 (200 Kick/200 Free) @ :20 rest
#3 (200 Choice/200 Kick no board)

1 x 300 Scull
4 x 50 Dolphin on Back @ :50

4 x 100 (Kick/Drill) Worst Stroke @ 1:50
1 x 700 Paddle/Pull

    SPRINT

4 x {
   1 x 75 MAX
   :30 rest
   50 MAX from push
}

1 x 300 Easy
2 x 200 @ 2:30
White-Pink
8 x 25 w/fins Underwater @ :40

    DISTANCE

4 x 100 IM @ 1:50 Pink

12 x 50 Fins @ :40
4 x 50 #1 drill, #2 build, #3 drill, #4 sprint @ :30

3 x { – 2 Minutes between each round
300 White @ 3:50/4:00
2 x 75 Pink @ 1:10/1:15
4 x 100 Red @ 1:10/1:15
2 x 25 MAX @ :40
}

    MID-DISTANCE

4 x 200 @ 2:40/2:50
Descend Each 200 + 25 Blue
(1:00)
4 x 300 @ 4:10/4:20
Each 300 - 100 Pull no buoy, 100 Build , 100 MAX Kick
(1:00)
10 x 100 @ 1:25/1:30
Hold Best Average
(2:00)
8 x 100 @ 1:10

Tue Feb 22 2022

1 x 100 SKIMPS

4 x 50 kick no board #1 stroke @ :50

4 x 100 IMO (Kick/Drill/Swim/Drill) @ 2:20
3 x 200 Free
4 x 25 kick red @ :30

IM
3 x 300 IMO by 75's @ :20 Rest

4 x 100 IM JMI @ 1:20/1:30
(:30)
4 x 100 IMO @ 1:30/1:40
Descend
(1:00)
8 x 50 Hold Goal Pace 200 +1 Same Stroke @ 1:00

Wed Feb 23 2022

4 x 200
#1 Free #2 Back/Breast by 50's #3 100 BK/100 Choice #4 Free
1 x 300 Kick
2 x 200 (100 White/100 Red Kick @ 3:30
6 x 50 D1-3 to Pink, 4-6 to MAX (start at White) @ 1:00

8 x 100 @ 1:40
#1-3 (50 Kick Red/50 Kick White)
#4-7 (75 Kick Pink/25 Kick MAX)
#8 100 Kick MAX

    SPRINT

6 x 100 (white-pink-red-blue) @ 1:15

8 x 25@ 1:00 rest

1 x 100 Broken @ the 50 and the 75 @ 4:00 rest
2 x 50 MAX from a dive @ 2:30 rest

1 x 200 White
4 x 100 Kick D 1-4@ 1:45
5 x 50 (25 kick/25 swim) @ 1:00

    DISTANCE

3 x (300 + 100 easy)
#1 Paddle/Pull White
#2 Paddle Pink
#3 Swim Red

4 x (200 + 100 easy)
White-Pink-Red-Blue
5 x (100 + 50 easy)
#1 Stroke D1-5 to MAX

3 x 200 Paddle DPS @ 2:20/2:25

    MID-DISTANCE

8 x 100 Paddle/Pull @ 1:20/1:30

3 x (300 + 100 easy)
White-Pink-Red
(2:00
8 x (75 + 25 easy)
White-Pink-Red-White x 2

10 x (50 + 50 easy)
Hold 500 Goal pace

Thu Feb 24 2022

4 x 200 Paddle w/Pull Buoy @ 2:20/2:30/2:40

1 x 400 Kick
4 x 100 Kick (50 pink/50 red) @ 1:50
4 x 50 MAX Kick @ 1:00
1 x 200 easy

5 x 100 @ 1:25/1:30
Descend 1-5

2 x {
   4 x 100
   odds: Free @ 1:45/1:50
   evens: Non-Free – Pink @ 1:50/2:00
   4 x 50 @ :40
}

Fri Feb 25 2022

600 Free
3 x 100 Kick w/Board
10 x 100 IM Order @ :15 rest

2 x {
   4 x 25 fist drill
   2 x 25 Stroke build
}
4x 25 (drill/build/drill/sprint) @ :40

     SPRINT

6 x 12.5 MAX

2 x (300 + 100 easy)
#1 Work Turns & MAX Breakout
#2 Great Finish MAX @ every wall
(1:00)
4 x (100 + 50 easy)
(2) White (2) Pink
8 x (50 + 50 easy)
#1-4 200 Best Time
#5-8 Hold Goal 200 Pace −1

     DISTANCE

12 x 75 (2 easy @ 1:10, 1 FAST @ 1:00)

1 x 600 Pull @ 7:00/7:50
4 x 75 Kick @ 1:20
odds: White-Pink-Red
Evens: Red-Pink-White
(1:00)
1 x 600 Pull @ 6:50/7:40
4 x 100 Kick @ 1:30/1:40
Descend to MAX start @ Pink
(2:00)
2 x 500 Swim @ 5:20/5:40
(2:00)
4 x 200 Swim w/fins @ 2:15

     MID-DISTANCE

4 x { 1-White, 2-Pink, 3-Red, 4-Blue
   1 x (500 + 100 easy)
   4 x (50 + 50) MAX
}

Sat Feb 26 2022

1 x 200 Kick Breast
1 x 200 Kick Fly
1 x 200 Back
1 x 200 Kick Free

3 x 300 @ 3:45/3:55
(1:00)
8 x 25 Paddles DPS – Count Stroke per 25 @ :45
4 x 25 Keep Same Stroke Count as w/ paddles per 25

5 x 50 drill @ 1:00

4 x 25 Kick Build each 25 @ :40
4 x 50 Kick Descend @ :55
4 x 25 Kick @ :30

9 x 50 (2 @ :40, 1 @ :30)

1 x 600 Free
1 x 400 RIMO drill/swim
1 x 200 Non-Free
8 x 50 2 each Stroke drill/swim @ :10 rest
1 x 600 Paddle/Pull
1 x 200 choice
6 x 100 @ 1:10/1:15
Keep all the same speed

Mon Feb 28 2022

2 x 300
#1 Free #2 RIMO (drill fly)
6 x 50 non-free @ :15 rest
5 x 100 Paddle w/Pull Buoy @ 1:30
6 x 50 Pull @ 1:00

2 x {
   3 x 50 fist drill @ 1:00
   8 x 25 #1 Stroke drill @ :45
   4 x 25 build @ :30
}
4 x 100 (50 #1 Stroke/50 Free) @ 1:30
 Stroke – easy free

   SPRINT

6 x 100 @ 1:30/1:40
Descend each 100
(1:00)
8 x 75 @ :55/1:00
(2:00)
6 x 150 @ 2:00/2:10
#1-3 Negative Split
#4-6 Best average
(2:00)
5 x 100 JMI @ 1:00/1:05/1:10

   DISTANCE

5 x 100 D1-5
5 x 100 Neg Split (Clear-Pink) @ 1:30

4 x 75 MAX @ 5:00
4 x 50 MAX @ 3:00

1 x 400 easy

2 x (5 x 50 @ 1:30) ALL OUT MAX

   MID-DISTANCE

8 x 75 (drill/swim/drill) @ 1:15

8 x 50 Kick D 1-4 , 5-8 to MAX @ 1:00
4 x 300 White @ 3:50/4;00
4 x 250 White @ 3:00/3:30
4 x 200 Pink @ 2:30/2:40/2:50
4 x 100 Red @ 1:10/1:15/1:20
8 x 50 @ :40 JMI

Manufactured by Amazon.ca
Bolton, ON